Strategic Interaction

CAMBRIDGE LANGUAGE TEACHING LIBRARY

A series covering central issues in langauge teaching and learning, by authors who have expert knowledge in their field.

In this series:

Strategic Interaction

Learning languages through scenarios

Robert J. Di Pietro

University of Delaware

Originally published in The New Directions
in Language Teaching Series, edited by
Howard B. Altman and Peter Strevens

CAMBRIDGE
UNIVERSITY PRESS

Published by the Press Syndicate of the University of Cambridge
The Pitt Building, Trumpington Street, Cambridge CB2 1RP
40 West 20th Street, New York, NY 10011-4211, USA
10 Stamford Road, Oakleigh, Melborne 3166, Australia

First published 1987
Fourth printing 1994

Printed in the United States of America

Library of Congress Cataloging-in Publication Data is availale

A catalogue record for this book is available from the British Library

ISBN 0-521-32425-4 hardback
ISBN 0-521-31197-7 paperback

Contents

Preface

Learning a new language should be as meaningful as any other social activity. It should entail the same dynamic tension that enlivens real-life encounters. If it is too much to expect that mastering the routine of everyday existence in a new language will always be highly motivating, a genuine excitement is generated when learners are faced with the need to handle the unexpected. In such situations, the pathway to resolution is not necessarily evident. Faced with an uncertainty of outcome in dealing with others, an individual's use of the new language necessarily takes on a strategic value. Words become more than conveyors of information. They assume a tactical worth that can be assessed only in terms of how well they contribute to gaining one's goals. Most people are probably not conscious of the strategic nature of what they say in their own language. With varying degrees of success, they talk their way through interactions with overeager sales personnel and uncooperative waiters. However, people are not so readily successful when they find themselves in a foreign country where their lack of verbal proficiency makes such basic interactions difficult and clumsy.

The approach to second-language instruction presented in this book attempts to turn such situations to an advantage by bringing them into the classroom and building a pedagogy around them. The term "scenario" will be used to give a label to real-life happenings that entail the unexpected and require the use of language to resolve them. The approach organized around scenarios is called "strategic interaction" (SI), to feature the way it calls upon learners to invoke the target language purposefully and artfully in dealing with others.[1]

The classroom can become an ideal location for this kind of approach.[2] There, we can re-create the conditions of social life and provide our students with the help and guidance they need to deal with them. We can also arrange our activities so that students are given optimal control

---

1 J. T. Roberts (1982) provides an excellent overview of strategic interaction together with a presentation of other approaches to second-language instruction. Titone (1982) recognizes the importance of interpersonal interaction in the classroom and the need to break away from viewing language teaching as information transmission.
2 For further clarification of the term "approach" as it is used in this book see Richards and Rodgers (1982). The reader may also wish to consult Anthony (1963) for another definition of the term.

over their own learning of the target language. The classroom can harbor a community of people who are, at the same time, learners and users of a new language. In the philosophy behind the strategic interaction approach, it is as users of the new language that people become learners of it.

In order to weld the learning of a new language to its use, strategic interaction puts students through three diverse kinds of classroom activities: rehearsal, performance, and debriefing. The *rehearsal* activity allows students to work together in groups to explore possible solutions to the situation of the scenario that has been assigned to them. *Performances* by individual students follow rehearsals. Performing students are free to interrupt their discourse in order to return to their rehearsal groups for impromptu consultations whenever they reach an impasse. *Debriefing* follows performance and engages the entire class in a discussion of any aspect of the scenario and its execution they wish to discuss. Details of how scenarios are prepared and how the class moves through rehearsal, performance, and debriefing will be spelled out in Chapters 1–5; how strategic interaction addresses the four audiolingual skills, the evaluation of student progress, the teaching of literature, and the training of teachers will also be treated.

A word is in order about the spirit in which this book was written. In addition to wanting to show how new languages can be learned through lifelike interactions in scenarios, I also wanted to assist classroom teachers to realize the full potential of their own creativity with the language they are teaching. As the reader will witness in the pages of this book, scenario themes can be as provocative and stimulating to teachers as they are to students. There is rarely a single solution to a scenario, and each scenario performance is different from all others. Each class meeting becomes a refreshing experience for the teacher as well as for the students. The refreshed teacher is an enthusiastic one, and enthusiasm is infectious within the restricted space of a language classroom. At the same time, I am aware of the many constraints of curriculum and time under which all practicing language teachers must work. In light of different instructional settings, it may not be possible to employ the techniques of strategic interaction to their fullest extent. I am confident, however, that those teachers who are able to set aside a session or two to try out the approach will find their appetites sufficiently whetted to want to do more.

There are many who contributed in some way or another to the writing of this book and the articulation of the approach. My gratitude goes to all those students at the University of Delaware and elsewhere who participated in strategic interaction demonstrations and lessons. There are far too many of them to thank personally. I am also very grateful to several national and international organizations that provided the opportunity to develop the approach through seminars, workshops, and inservices: The United States Information Agency (USIA), the Goethe Institute of New York, the Japan Association of College English Teachers (JACET), the Horwood Language Centre (Melbourne, Australia), the Australian National University (Canberra), IDRA of San Antonio, Texas, and the National Training Resource Center of San Diego State University, California. Many colleagues both in the United States and abroad have added substantially to my thinking through their discussions with me and their writings: Frederick J. Bosco, Margarita Calderón, Marcel Danesi, Sara Jane DiLaura Morris, Rick Donato, William Frawley, Rajai Khanji, Angela Labarca, James Lantolf, Don McCreary, Carol Puhl, Terry Quinn, John T. Roberts, Olga Rubio, and Ghaida Salah. I am cognizant of the contribution made by those teachers at the University of Delaware who were willing to try out my ideas: Joan Brown, Flora Calabrese, Rene Coulet du Gard, Debbie Coen, Mary Donaldson-Evans, Gabriella Finizio, Rebecca Pauly, Bonnie Robb, and Eugenia Slavov. A special word of thanks goes to Deryn P. Verity, who read and commented on two drafts of the manuscript and contributed significantly to its final articulation. Howard B. Altman, New Directions in Language Teaching series editor, and Ellen Shaw of Cambridge University Press were especially generous not only in guidance and advice but also in showing much patience with me as I labored on the manuscript. I am also grateful to Sandra Graham at Cambridge University Press for the fine job of copyediting the manuscript.

1 The beginnings of an interactive approach

A spoken message at the time it is needed, no matter how imperfect, is worth many unspoken messages, no matter how perfect.

Rubin and Thompson (1982: 66)

Imagine you are about to return home from a trip abroad. You reach the check-in counter at the airport where you expect to go through the usual formalities of baggage checking and seat assignment. Instead, the airline clerk informs you that your flight has been overbooked. He offers you $100 and full compensation for the cost of staying over one more night if you will take a flight tomorrow. The offer is attractive but you have been caught off-guard. You need time to think. Classes are about to start and, as a teacher, you were counting on having a day to prepare lessons for the first week. A friend of yours has agreed to meet you at the airport back home. You need to ask the clerk some questions: If I change my ticket, what assurances will I have of a seat on tomorrow's flight? Will the airline send a telegram to inform my friend of my new date and time of arrival?

Whether you like it or not, you have been thrust into a real-life situation. You must decide a matter that will affect how you will live the next twenty-four hours of your life. Perhaps the furthest thought from your mind is the instructional potential that derives from this situation. Yet there is something to be learned from having to find a resolution to it. You will be engaging in a conversation – either in your own language or in the one spoken in this country – that may be unlike any other you ever had. How good it would be to have a friend or two by your side to advise you as you speak with the airline clerk.

Students who are learning a new language through the strategic interaction approach are placed in situations, or scenarios, like the one described here. Unlike real life, however, they are given the opportunity to discuss their options and plan their strategies in groups (the rehearsal phase) before having to face the other party in the scenario (the performance phase). They are even permitted to interrupt their conversation and return to their supporting groups if they feel the need for on-the-spot help. As a final boost to learning through the scenario experience, the entire class is taken through a debriefing after the performance of the role players. During this time, discussion can range from choice of strategies to matters of style, grammar, pronunciation,

1

and vocabulary. Teacher preparation and teacher–student participation in each of the three phases of strategic interaction can be outlined as follows:

Pre-class Preparation:
  Teacher selects or creates appropriate scenarios and prepares the necessary role cards.
Phase 1 (Rehearsal):
  Students form groups and prepare agendas to fulfill the roles assigned to them. Teacher acts as adviser and guide to student groups as needed.
Phase 2 (Performance):
  Students perform their roles with support of their respective groups while teacher and remainder of class look on.
Phase 3 (Debriefing):
  Teacher leads the entire class in a discussion of the students' performance.

A repertory of effective scenarios is vital to the strategic interaction approach. The essential ingredients of a scenario are discussed at the start of Chapter 3. For now, it is enough to think of the scenario as a classroom activity that motivates students to converse purposefully with each other by casting them in roles in episodes based on or taken from real life. When successful, the scenario promotes dramatic tension among the role players. This tension results from requiring that the players determine the outcome. In a classroom adaptation of the situation of the overbooked flight, for example, no particular plan of action would be recommended to either party. The "traveler" would be left to weigh the advantages and disadvantages of a delayed return flight, and the "airline clerk" would have to decide on what concessions to make to the "traveler." The indeterminacy of outcome leads the role players to concentrate on using the target language as strategically as possible as they decide on a position and then articulate it. In an important way, the students are playing themselves in exercising their roles. They are free to make their own choices about what to say and, in doing so, to find the language needed to express those choices. The open-endedness of scenario solutions is even carried over to the debriefing session that follows the performance. During the debriefing, the entire class is invited to propose alternative solutions to the scenario and to discuss how these solutions might come about.

The intention at this point is to provide only essential information about the strategic interaction approach so that the background presented in this chapter will be coherent. Questions about how to prepare scenarios and how to be most effective in orchestrating the three phases of strategic interaction will be answered in the chapters that follow. It is important to understand that strategic interaction not only uses lifelike situations, it also gives learners a way to be full participants in human discourse, even though that discourse may take place in a language they are only beginning to learn. Experienced language teachers know that to become accurate and fluent in a new language requires competencies beyond the bits and pieces of grammar and vocabulary that are highlighted in textbooks. The successful learner responds to the demands of interaction with speakers of the language in ways that we all recognize but have difficulty reducing to formal classroom exercises. Strategic interaction, with its use of scenarios, allows learners to rise to the challenge of human interaction, with all its uncertainties and ambiguities. An important first step to successful implementation of strategic interaction is taken when the teacher recognizes that the dramatic nature of human interactions can be the key to addressing all of the essentials without having to make each one explicit at all times.

The drama of human interactions

The well-written scenario captures the dramatic element of a human interaction and, in doing so, enhances retention of what is learned when that interaction is performed. People who have lived or traveled in countries where they do not speak the language often attest to the effectiveness of dramatic episodes in learning the language. An acquaintance who had visited Cairo, Egypt, could still say, twenty years after her stay there, the Arabic equivalent of "There's water on the bathroom floor." She had put this utterance together in response to a real need to describe a state of affairs in her hotel room. There is no doubt that her success in communicating with the desk clerk helped to fix the utterance forever in her mind. We could go on to conjecture about the psychological processes that were put into play. Or we might say simply that the urgency of the situation had triggered her "language acquisition device" so that it produced an intelligible sentence from the rudiments of Arabic that she had already acquired. As teachers of languages we would do well to explore the ways in which similar moments of dramatic tension can be created in the classroom and used to stimulate lively performances in the target language. Without the element of dramatic tension, a scenario is not likely to be successful, no matter how relevant its theme might be to learners' functional needs.

Sometimes the dramatic tension is locked within the students' own experiences, as I discovered some fifteen years ago. I was teaching a course in conversational Italian at the time. All of the students happened to be young women who had spent their junior year of college studying in Italy. The class was supposed to be an advanced one – which made the choice of materials particularly difficult. Eventually a text was found

3

and we went through the dialogs in each chapter. It became clear after only a few meetings that the students were bored. The textbook dialogs were stilted and unoriginal. In an effort to rescue the class from total failure, I suggested that the students write their own dialogs and perform them in class. The turnabout was astounding. The level of motivation took a marked upswing and the dialogs written by the students were lively and believable. These women used the dialogs to discuss their dealings with young men and the problems they had fending off undesired suitors. They wrote about their experiences with unfamiliar foods and their efforts not to offend their hosts. They eagerly consulted me about things they might have said in these situations. They were especially interested in how people can use language to gain their own ends. They gave advice to each other about how to handle difficult situations. I came to realize that I had probably selected the text as a traditional middle-aged male teacher, seeing Italy through my own particular filter. The author of the text must have been of a similar orientation. Thanks to my students' discourse, my filter was lowered and I caught a glimpse of life in an Italian setting as a woman in her twenties might experience it. The class became exciting and different for me. I became more of a counselor than an imparter of invariable truisms about Italian. I came to realize that I could not represent all ages or life-styles in an Italian speech community, and perhaps I should not even try to do so.

Of course, there were problems in using a similar technique with other foreign-language classes, at lower levels, where the students had not already lived abroad. I wondered how the use of dramatic dialog could be reconciled with the need to acquire so much unfamiliar grammar. It was easier to involve the students in talking about real-life experiences in an ESL class I taught. Even there, however, I could not find a way to integrate this activity with all the other exercises prescribed by the text and the syllabus. The solutions to these problems were to come many years later, when I was finally able to achieve the full reorientation needed to both the practice of teaching foreign languages and the theoretical models that underlie how they are learned.

The linguistic components of the self

An important step to the required reorientation was taken when I realized how centrally language functions in creating the perception of a "self." My training as a linguist had led me to concentrate on language as an artifact built by its own set of rules. The ways in which language serves to make a statement about the individuals who use it were regrettably not within my usual realm of investigation. Then a student told me about an experience he had had in the Netherlands. This young man had been born in Argentina, of Dutch parentage. He grew up speaking Dutch at home and Spanish elsewhere. At the age of twenty, he took a trip to the Netherlands – his very first visit to the land of his parents' birth. His command of Dutch was excellent, as far as grammar and pronunciation were concerned. Since he had not experienced life in a community where only Dutch was spoken, however, he had not learned how to function in such a setting. He made *faux pas*, he asked disarming questions about the most basic of cultural and social matters. He recalled that one native became especially nonplussed when he asked, in perfectly articulated Dutch, "What does a mailbox look like?" Eventually, he found a way to play a socially more appropriate role: He developed a foreign accent. Now whenever he asked questions, such as what end of the bus to get on, people accepted him as someone who was not one of them. He could make social blunders without being taken as insane. His accent fit his set of circumstances much better than fluency in the language. He was no longer expected to possess the knowledge that fluent Dutch-speaking people have about their culture and society.

Accent and grammatical accuracy play important parts in establishing identities in a foreign language. Yet sounding native can have relatively little to do with successful interaction with the alien society. It is not unusual to find foreigners who are far from accurate in their use of the new language but can, nevertheless, function in society.[1] Indeed, the skill of the young Dutch speaker from Argentina was considerable but still did not allow him to function comfortably in a Dutch-speaking community. Certainly this should indicate that acquiring a nativelike accent is not the best or only goal. It is highly likely that individual differences in how roles are interpreted in the alien setting contribute significantly to accent. We have known for some time that individual students respond in diverse ways to the need to articulate the sounds of the target language (Neufield 1979). Rather than look exclusively for a physiological basis to these differences (labeling some students more "skillful" than others), we might explore the impact that making new language sounds has on the human psyche. As illustrated by the example of the Dutch speaker, speaking a language with nativelike accuracy implies a commitment of personal integration with the native speakers of that language. Maintaining an accent of some sort can serve as a communicative "shield," protecting the nonnative from having to display total knowledge of or commitment to the target-language community. Such shields are not

1 Some very interesting research has been done on the relationship of language to personality, especially as it affects the acquisition of nativelike pronunciation in foreign languages. The work of Alexander Guiora and his associates is especially prominent in this area (see, for example, Guiora and Acton 1979).

only found among adult learners; there is evidence that even children may develop shields when faced with living in foreign settings (see Wong Fillmore 1976). In any event, we should avoid simplistic explanations of the inability to develop "good" accents on the basis of maturation or setting. As far as implications for a teaching methodology are concerned, we should take the issue of self, that is, personal identity, into account when evaluating the target language performances of our students. In an interactive classroom – one in which students use the target language to interact in personally meaningful ways – the factor of intelligibility comes into play. Learners who are called upon to express personal desires or views and to negotiate with classmates will develop enough accuracy of pronunciation and grammar to be understood. The need to interact is a factor in this development. Whether or not the individual student becomes nativelike in pronunciation and grammar may depend largely on the way in which that student constructs a new identity in the foreign language. The interactive teacher is sensitive to the developing identity of each student and should understand that a nativelike command of the language may not be a realistic goal for some.

The three dimensions of language

The multiple concerns with how language is patterned grammatically, how it is used by people to negotiate with others, and how it serves its users in creating personal identities suggest three distinct dimensions to be covered by scenarios:

1. *Information exchange* (with its grammatical orientation);
2. *Transaction* (with its focus on negotiation and the expression of speaker intentions);
3. *Interaction* (with an emphasis on how language works to portray roles and speaker identities).

The details of each dimension will be taken up in subsequent chapters, but for now a brief introduction to each will suffice to orient the teacher to what is needed in the implementation of scenarios.

The dimension best known to language teachers is that of information exchange. We can illustrate how this dimension operates by taking a pair of utterances in a dialog such as the following:

A: Can you tell me what time this train gets to New York?
B: Around 7 P.M., I think.

To understand the information in the dialog, students need to know that A has asked a question about the time of the train's arrival and B has supplied an answer. The traditional way of talking about this interaction is to describe its structure. For example, A has formed the question by initiating it with a modal auxiliary and by using the question word "what" later on in the sentence. B's response is a prepositional phrase followed by a short declarative (subject/verb). In making observations about the structure of the two utterances we are operating in the realm of grammar, which is built upon the way information is structured in a language.

Moving to the dimension of transaction, we shift our focus to the intent of what is said. We delve beneath the meanings of the words and their grammatical arrangement to investigate the purposes that the speakers may be attaching to what they are saying to each other. How will B interpret the intent of A's utterance in the sample dialog? Will B decide that it is nothing more than a request for information? A may already know what time the train is supposed to arrive in New York and wishes, instead, to pass the time away on a long and boring voyage by initiating conversation with B. It will be B's task to interpret A's intention and then decide on a response to give. In working out the transactions of a dialog, we need to consider setting and nonverbal elements, such as the intonation used, the facial expressions, and the accompanying gestures, if any. If B interprets A's question as an invitation to chat and wishes to accept it as such, B can express that acceptance in a number of ways, such as by a friendly tone of voice and a smile. A decision not to accept such an overture can also be signaled in various ways, such as avoidance of eye contact, falling intonation, and/or a lack of facial expression.

Whereas a consideration of transactions entails how speakers use language to express their intentions and attain their goals, a study of interactions leads us to analyze the ways in which the speakers use language to enact roles. These roles include the overt ones of "information seeker" and "information giver" that are apparent in our illustrative dialog. Depending on the nature of the discourse, they might also include the less overt kinds of roles that can grow between traveling companions, such as "friend," "confidant," "debating partner," or even "competitor" (if, for example, both turn out to be salespersons for rival companies). In any event, proficient speakers are expected to be able to associate what is said to one or more of these probable roles.

We cannot expect learners to be able to discern all significant roles they encounter through conversations in the target language. However, we can hope that learners will pay some attention to expressions that clearly demarcate social roles, such as "Can I help you?" which is a characteristic opener for sales clerks in North American department stores. The rejoinder "Just looking" is an equally typical expression of someone who does not wish to assume the complementary role of "customer," preferring, instead, to be a "window-shopper." The pairing of "sales clerk" with "customer" or "window-shopper" illustrates the complementary feature of roles, namely that they function in pairs.

In a perfect world – as well as in some language classes – interactions run in total harmony because the roles being played are in full complementation. The ideal sales clerk finds the ideal customer to whom to sell the desired product. On the occasions that such interactions are found in real life, it is possible to predict almost fully what each person will say to the other. In the classroom, the level of predictability is even higher whenever students are required to recite prepared dialogs.

The relevance of ambiguity to discourse

The concept of structural ambiguity gained notoriety around 1960 when it was introduced into linguistics through transformational grammar. According to the transformationalists, a grammar of a language should be able to disambiguate sentences, that is, give a structural explication of "underlying" meanings. Sentences like "Flying planes can be dangerous" were shown to have several different meanings by applying transformations and turning up such paraphrases as "Planes that fly are dangerous" or "The flying of planes is dangerous."

As important as it might be to discern ambiguity in the structure of sentences such as this one, other ambiguities in the dimensions of transaction and interaction are probably of even greater significance for speakers of a language. In natural discourse, each participant is led to attach meanings to utterances beyond the meaning of their factual content. The statement "It's cold in here" may be a simple acknowledgment of a state of affairs, but the intent of the person who made the declaration is open to interpretation by those who hear it. Perhaps the speaker would like to be given a sweater. Perhaps the speaker's intent is to have someone turn up the heat. There are other potential transactional interpretations, depending on what experience has been shared by the speakers and what the hearers decide is the proper one. Someone may say or do something in return that is not in line with what the speaker originally intended. The comment about the ambient temperature may have been intended metaphorically, to describe a sense of hostility that is present between two individuals in the room who have just had an argument. Whatever the case, the need to uncover the agendas of those contributing to the discourse is more important than disambiguating the structure of the initial statement.

The interactive type of ambiguity relates to how each interacting party perceives the roles being played by the others. Aside from roles that are clearly marked either by conventionalized utterances (such as the overture "Can I help you?" from the shopkeeper) or by clothing (as when store employees wear special jackets), there is ample room for uncertainty as to what psychological roles are being played in a conversation. Is this person really trying to be my benefactor? Will I be led to commit myself to buying something that is not useful? Used-car dealers in the United States often assume titles like Uncle Bill or Cousin Ted in order to project a familial – and therefore trustworthy – role when dealing with potential customers.

In keeping with our multidimensional view of language, each type of ambiguity fits into a particular dimension of language: structural ambiguity in the dimension of information exchange, and transactional and interactive ambiguity in the dimensions of transaction and interaction. Although the teacher is advised to look for all three types of ambiguity and note the effects they have on student performances in the target language, ambiguity is not necessarily a bad feature of natural speech. Being intentionally vague can help achieve one's desired goals in conversation. Uncertainty about strategies used and roles being played is probably present in much of what people say to each other every day. As language teachers we have traditionally urged our students to be "clear" and "precise" about what they want to say in the target language. Perhaps we should be more realistic and look for ways in which lack of information or uncertainty about the intentions of others can motivate people to use the target language skillfully. The scenario as set forth in Chapter 3 is especially effective in prompting learners to interact with each other without the full knowledge (and with possible misunderstanding) of what each is trying to say. Being required to interpret (or "disambiguate") the intentions of others and to plot out new utterances that advance one's own purposes leads the learners to attend to all three dimensions of conversation in the target language.

The rationale for an interactive approach

To be well acquainted with an approach requires an understanding of the theories of language and language acquisition that underlie it, together with the general principles that motivate each aspect of its techniques. This knowledge is necessary if the teacher is to develop new materials and variations that stand within its general confines.

The overall framework of strategic interaction is built upon the following:

1. the expectation that learners will work toward fulfillment of personal agendas in conversation as the purpose for generating discourse;

2. the stimulation in the classroom of lifelike situations in which personal agendas can be invoked;
3. the derivation of explanations and/or drills from utterances either created by the students themselves or given to them in order to expand utterances created by them; all target-language performances are to take place in a context that is meaningful to the learners;
4. the acceptance of participatory discourse, complete with its non-verbal components, as the basic subject matter to be taught (as opposed to decontextualized sentences based on grammar or vocabulary alone);
5. the development of testing instruments that address language in all its dimensions of use rather than in terms of discrete points;
6. the recognition that a teacher's control of the instructional process is not equivalent to dominance over the learners' efforts to gain competence in the target language (i.e., the students' learning is under their own control).

Insofar as other approaches are motivated by criteria similar to those listed here, they are compatible with strategic interaction. For example, strategic interaction has the group orientation of Community Language Learning, the respect for receptive learning of the Natural Approach, and the interactive tension of sociodrama. Role plays of various types also share some of the same motivating criteria as strategic interaction. Whatever its similarities with other approaches and techniques might be, strategic interaction relies very strongly on student-generated discourse as the focal point of classroom activity.

Strategic interaction starts with the premise that learning takes place only when the internal mind can be linked to the external world (see Donato 1985). It is through scenario dialogs that this linking is achieved. Learners are placed in situations where the motivation to think is translated into the challenge to reach goals through verbal exchanges with others. In an interactive approach, the classroom turns into a proving ground where such challenges are faced and overcome with the aid of the teacher and the cooperation of other learners. As Donato (1985) has pointed out for foreign-language learners and Crandall et al. (1985) have demonstrated for students of mathematics, the group in pooling its resources has greater knowledge than its individual members.

Since the agendas of diverse groups are brought into contact in the interactive classroom, discourse is better thought of as a manipulative act rather than as a cooperative one. Although the exchange of speech between individuals must adhere to general principles of conversational management in order to function (e.g., taking turns), the cooperative principle is more apparent than real (see, e.g., Goodwin 1981). As in any competitive sport, following the rules of the game is necessary to give structure to the encounter, but each side is playing to win and not simply to demonstrate how the game should be played.

The difference in mindset between teacher and students

To help clarify the role of the teacher in an interactive approach, it is necessary to realize that teachers are probably unlike most of the students they have in their classes, with regard to the task at hand. First of all, teachers – whether native or nonnative speakers of the target language – tend to identify themselves as representatives of the speakers of the target language. The usual goal of teachers is for students to strive to become fluent in the language (even though they recognize that such a goal is either very difficult or impossible to achieve). They place much emphasis on developing a near-nativelike pronunciation and a considerable vocabulary. These elements are easily noticed and evaluated in student performances. Teachers are also geared to listen attentively to the way the target language is performed. It appears that most people, other than teachers, do not attend to *how* something is being said but rather to *what* is being said; unless, of course, a foreign accent is so strong that the message becomes garbled. In contrast, teachers tend to focus on accuracy, eagerness to converse, and personality traits that seem most like their own.

Many students appear oriented in a different way toward learning a new language. They assume, perhaps naïvely, that they will ultimately be able to speak with natives as a result of their formal instruction. They have no idea of the considerable commitment of their egos that will be needed to achieve full communicative competence. Many students are "instrumentally" oriented toward language use. Such students do not want to remake themselves into neo-natives. They often believe the propaganda that learning a new language is a "broadening" experience, but they have no idea of how entangled they can become in matters of grammar before they can really "broaden" themselves.

These differences in mindset between teachers and students inevitably cause problems in teacher-centered approaches to foreign-language study. One learning style must be appropriate for all, and it must be compatible with the teacher's views. In an approach that allows students to control much of their own learning (as in strategic interaction), the two mindsets can exist in a pedagogical symbiosis. Such a symbiosis comes about when the teacher and the students both realize that the classroom is a kind of minor speech community where all play roles and

11

share in the instructional process. The teacher may orchestrate activities, but it is the students who fulfill them in their own ways.

A comment about reductionism

No field, especially one dealing with human behavior, advances when the whole is forgotten. Foreign-language teaching deals with the full range of human behavior and should be considered a behavioral discipline. If we concentrate on building classroom activities through recipes that deal with disjointed bits and pieces of language, we risk losing sight of our students as fellow humans committing themselves to one of the most engrossing endeavors anyone can undertake. It is important for us to remember that the basis of human interventions with language is not only cognitive, it is social and personal as well. To speak is to be human, and to learn how to speak a new language is to find new ways in which to express that same humanity. As humans we are naturally concerned with what we are saying and how we are accomplishing our purposes through language. Part of the training for teaching languages is to become attuned to *how* things are said. The language teacher must be attentive to details of form – there can be no question of that. What is of concern is how such details are addressed. In the approach presented in this book, all matters of detail about the target language and its use are couched within the context of discourse as generated by the students themselves. In this way, exercises and explanations on the most minute aspect of grammar will always lead back to the full act of speech, with all its dimensions. Through both rehearsal and debriefing phases of classroom activity, students are given the benefit of instructional guidance precisely where they feel it is needed as they prepare themselves to perform in the target language.

We can re-create in the classroom some important elements of target-language performance at the same time that we build our pedagogical treatment. We can isolate potentially stressful situations that come with real interactions with the language. We can bring these situations into the classroom and control them. In a way, the classroom can become a refuge for the learner. It is especially so in the case of ESL or any other language taught in a community where it is commonly spoken outside school walls. In a manner of speaking, formal classroom study of a new language serves a psychologically positive function by allowing students to work through potentially stressful situations as an integral part of the instructional process.

By interacting with each other through the target language, students pass through the steps that are necessary in personalizing any body of knowledge. These steps are clearly present in the unfolding of the interactive device that we have called the scenario (see Chapter 3 for a full discussion of the creation and use of the scenario):

1. appraise the situation;
2. consider what the options are for resolving it;
3. anticipate the responses of others in the chosen options;
4. apply the options by interacting with others in conversation;
5. review the results of the interaction and integrate the forthcoming information within a personal conceptual framework.

In following the five steps, students will find that the new language fulfills a natural function of all languages: It serves as a medium of communication and it carries individuals along a shared path of learning without cutting off the sources of personal gain from the experience.

The successful, or "good," language learner

There have been some attempts to postulate what makes a successful or good language learner. Rubin and Thompson (1982) posit a number of traits, such as willingness to take risks and the ability to paraphrase what is not well understood. Actually, the determination of success in the formal study of a second language depends on a number of variables beyond the students' personal characteristics. We should not assume that the world of second-language learners can be neatly divided into two camps of good and bad. Rather, let us start with the premise that anyone who is not suffering a learning disability is capable of successfully learning a foreign language. What factors, then, promote successful language learning?

Showstack (1982) suggests that formal classroom instruction of any kind may have a very small effect on the proficiency that the students eventually attain. According to Showstack, there are only two things that are clearly provided by the teacher: (1) exposure to the target language and (2) the motivation to continue studying the language. Perhaps the formal classroom is not the best place to learn a new language; but if we break away from the traditional idea of the teacher-dominated classroom, the classroom can become the locus of a functioning speech community in which natural discourse is simulated. At the University of Delaware, where both interactive and traditional language classes are held, it was observed that students enrolled in traditional classes who do poorly are likely to label themselves "poor" learners, whereas those enrolled in innovative classes are inclined to blame the teacher and/or the method for their lack of success. Perhaps the most reliable indicator of success in second-language learning is to be found in the student's willingness to extend the classroom experience

[handwritten margin note: interesting result!]

13

to interaction with speakers outside the classroom. For the successful second-language learner, formal instruction is only the start of a deepening involvement with speakers of the new language. As a result, measuring success must be a long-term affair and cannot be determined accurately within the time limitations of a semester or two of formal study.

A psychological basis for interactive second-language instruction

It is possible to associate most second-language approaches and methodologies with a psychological model of language learning. The writings of Lev Semenovich Vygotsky provide such a model for the strategic interaction approach to second-language instruction. According to Vygotsky, individuals develop thinking processes through dialog with other individuals (see especially Vygotsky 1962, 1978). Society and the group are sources of creativity that foster new ideas and provide solutions to problems. He describes three types of regulation that speakers undergo in their use of language:

1. *Object*-regulation, whereby a person's verbal performance is dominated by a concern to adhere to the rules and conventions of the language. Learners who are overly regulated by the object of language are unable to express their own thoughts or to respond adequately to the verbal performance of others.[2]
2. *Other*-regulation, marking the situation in which someone's verbal performance is dictated by the remarks and commentary of other speakers (as when the learners use most of their verbal output to answer questions or perform drills directed by the teacher).
3. *Self*-regulation, when speakers feel unrestrained in conveying their own thoughts and desires (clearly an admirable goal to achieve in second-language instruction, although over-self-regulation can result in incoherent speech, since the over-self-regulated individual is apt to pay little attention to either the specific rules of the grammar or the conversational conventions by which people try to make themselves understood to others).

2 With reference to over-regulation by the object, Brumfit (1980) has already recognized the need to abandon syllabi that concentrate on the target language as a product. Even syllabi of functions and notions are liable to foster over-regulation by the object. Teachers should probably continue to develop artifactual syllabi but should take care not to let them dominate the instructional process. Alan Maley (1980) adds to Brumfit's criticism of syllabi with the observation that a communicative approach to language teaching necessarily entails a commitment to dealing with reality.

The three types of regulation reflect the three key elements present in a second-language classroom: the language to be learned, the teacher, and the individuals learning the language. Through the dynamics of dialogic speech, learners are given the opportunity to reach a balance of the three. Since the teacher and members of the class share in other-regulation, the tendency toward overuse of this type of regulation is avoided.

Summary

Second-language learning is a humanistic undertaking. It involves human beings in all the ways that characterize human interactions. The ultimate worth of second-language methodologies and approaches is to be found in how well learners are able to extend their classroom experience to discourse outside the instructional framework. In the classroom, the teacher cannot presume to dominate learning. A recognition should be made of the differences in mindset about second-language learning found among the students. By making interactive discourse the basic activity, the teacher is able to provide the variety of guidance and explanation that is likely to meet the needs of individual students. Collaboration in groups enables students to build the parts of dialogs in the target language and acquire the competence needed to do so. By fostering an interactive tension through scenarios, the teacher leads the students to discover aspects of the target language needed to resolve the tension.

The achievement of a nativelike accent is an unrealistic goal for the classroom. It is often not needed in order to communicate one's message adequately to speakers of the target language, in any event. Students fit their use of the target language to their particular choice of identities. A foreign accent may actually become a shield for them as they interact with speakers of the target language. Interactive proficiency is expressed in the three dimensions of information exchange, transaction, and interaction. All natural discourse contains these three dimensions and therefore should be simulated in the classroom.

The distinction between "good" and "bad" second-language learners is questioned. Among the variables that affect the success or failure of second-language learners are the teacher and the method or approach. Following the Vygotskyan model of learning, students are regulated by three factors: the object (i.e., the forms and structures of the target language), the other (the teacher and others in the class), and the self (each learner). The teacher should take special care to provide the kind of other-regulation that is most helpful to the student. By engaging the students in dialogs, the teacher helps to achieve a balance of all three regulatory forces.

[handwritten margin note: possible but not necessarily so!]

15

2 The first day...and all that follow

The first meeting of any language class should be exciting. Not knowing precisely what is to come sharpens everyone's expectations. How difficult will this class be? Will I be a successful learner? How effective will this teacher be? The assumption is that everyone – students and teacher alike – will make every effort to get off to a good start. The teacher comes into the room, glances at the students, and stands in front of the class. What will the teacher's first words be? A salutation, perhaps: ¡Buenos días! ('Good morning!'). No response is expected, of course. The students have just taken the very first steps on a long voyage into the mysteries of a new language.

The classroom is an instructional setting. It is a place where the activity of teaching can be observed. Learning, too, is supposed to happen there, but that is not so easily observed. Even the teacher of a second language (i.e., of a language spoken in the surrounding community) engages in a fiction about discourse. In the classroom, what is said in the target language is for display purposes, to illustrate the forms and structures of the target language. The teacher is not only the model but also the judge of what is proper and correct in the target language. The sample utterances in the textbook are also part of the fiction. They are well-formed, but most were probably never said by any real person for any real purpose. Sooner or later, the students come to accept the artificiality of the classroom routine because it is safer to do so than to try to use the new language for real purposes. Many will attempt to conform to what is expected of them and what will be the basis for evaluation and grading.

The term "coverage" has had great currency among language teachers. When do we "cover" the future tense? How can the subjunctive be "covered?" Teachers work according to syllabi and course outlines based on grammar and vocabulary. Not to cover all the points in the syllabus is unpardonable for some school administrators. If teachers dare to try something new in class, they had better make certain that the syllabus is covered or else they will incur the disapproval of the authorities and become known as the teachers who cannot "get through the syllabus."

When the routine becomes overbearing, teachers may look for ways to make classroom activities more "natural." They may engage their students in brief role plays. Perhaps the teacher will dramatize a per-

16

sonage associated with the target culture, for example, Marie-Antoinette in a French class. The students are found to appreciate the extra effort being made by the teacher to relieve the drudgery of disciplined language study. In a less dramatic measure the teacher may attempt to conduct the class totally in the target language, using segments of contrived conversation to illustrate grammatical points. Leemann (1982: 272) provides the following sample of such an attempt in a French class:

Teacher: (*having already given the instruction to make a question out of a statement*) Je pense à mes amis de Paris – Joan?

Teacher: I'm thinking of my friends in Paris – Joan?

Joan: Um...à quoi pensez-vous?

Joan: Uh, what are you thinking about?

Teacher: Vous comprenez? (*teacher goes on to comment on the incorrect use of "quoi" by Joan*) Si vous considérez vos amis comme des objets (*laughing*) vous dites "quoi."

Teacher: Do you understand? If you think of your friends as objects, you say "quoi."

Joan: (*repeating*) Um, à quoi pensez-vous?

Joan: Uh, what are you thinking about?

Teacher: (*more excitedly*) Non, pas à quoi! Ils sont des personnes, n'est-ce pas? (*she then explains, in French, that "quoi" is for things and "qui" is for people*)

Teacher: No, not "à quoi"! They are people, aren't they?

Joan: (*in English*) Is it number six we're doing?

Teacher: Non, numéro sept, excusez-moi.

Teacher: No, number seven, excuse me.

Joan: Okay. A qui pensez-vous?

Joan: Okay. Who are you thinking about?

Poor Joan. Did she finally understand the difference between *qui* and *quoi*? How many more times will she confuse the two pronouns? In any event, the class is moving along smoothly and all units of the book are being covered. Some of the students in the class will be visiting France over the semester break. They should be ready to communicate with the French. Any mistakes made with *qui* and *quoi* will be their own fault.

We need not add further detail to our picture of a traditional second-language classroom, where language use is artificial and where everybody engages in producing mindless questions and answers. Eugene Ionesco could not have found greater inspiration elsewhere for his *Bald Soprano*, with its absurd dialog taken from the pages of an English textbook for foreigners!

Let us return to that first day of class and see if we can paint a brighter picture. We can start with the premise that the initial excitement of being in a language class should be somehow sustained throughout the course of instruction. Why, we can ask ourselves, must classroom activity become so routine and so artificial? Can we find a way to use language realistically and make our students look forward to each new lesson as if it were the first? Following is an illustration of a first day with the strategic interaction approach. The target language in this case is Italian.

Teacher: Buon giorno!

(This salutation is so closely tied to context that it is most likely comprehensible without any explanation.)

The teacher continues, in English or whatever language the students commonly speak:

Teacher: I am going to need some volunteers who would like to be transported, in their imaginations, to Rome.

Some students come forward, or the teacher selects some. The volunteers are asked to take seats placed in two rows, as if they were on a bus. One is asked to play the bus driver. The others are given no special assignments. The teacher then assumes the role of a new passenger entering the bus. Noticing a purse placed on a seat by one of the students, the teacher approaches and quickly snatches it, possibly without the owner noticing it.

Teacher: Well, now, who would like to say something about what happened? You may say whatever you wish, but it must be in Italian. Don't worry, I'll help you phrase it properly.

At this point, there may be some silence while each student thinks over the situation. Some students may choose to remain silent. Others will pick one of several options:

1. alert the victim;
2. shout at the bus driver to stop the bus;
3. address the thief directly;
4. make some remark about the situation to another passenger.

As the options are converted into Italian it will become obvious to the participants that some things are easier to say than others. For example, it is simpler to shout *Aiuto!* ('Help!') with no particular addressee in mind than to speak directly to the victim: "Mi scusi, Signora, ma qualcuno ha preso la Sua borsa" ('Excuse me, Ma'am, but someone has taken your purse'). Eventually, a dialog will take shape, with the teacher serving as informant. A sample dialog might go as follows:

Passenger 1: Aiuto! ('Help!')
Bus driver: Che è successo? ('What happened?')
Passenger 2: Al ladro! ('Stop, thief!')
Victim: Ha preso la mia borsa! ('He took my purse!')

This particular scenario has been tried many times, in many languages (Spanish, French, Italian, Dutch). Each time it is enacted there are slight variations, depending on the disposition of the students at the time of enactment. Some features are constant, whatever the variations:

1. The students choose brief utterances, usually of a direct-address form.
2. There is no constraint on who should be addressed (the victim, another passenger, the thief, the bus driver, etc.), and most of the time, several addressees (or none in particular) are intended.
3. The utterances are often accompanied by nonverbals. Depending on how aware the teacher is, nativelike gestures can be modeled along with the appropriate verbal content. In any event, the emergent dialog is replete with supporting kinesics.[1]

The performance phase of this scenario may continue with different students who might have alternative options they wish to try out. After the dialog has been generated (or while it is being generated), the teacher may write the utterances on the blackboard. Doing so helps the students to objectify the language and to prepare a corpus for the debriefing segment, which is the next phase. Rather than pick out one or two structural items that the teacher has preordained for discussion during debriefing, it is best to allow the students to ask their own questions. Inevitably, each has a particular concern: What is *la* in *la mia borsa*? What difference in pronunciation is there between the /s/ of *preso* and the /ss/ of *successo*? If the students have already had some instruction in another foreign language, they might ask questions like: If *ladro* and

---

1 Verity (1985) observes that the scenario about the purse snatcher on the bus corresponds to the demands of the bioprogram. That is, the language used in this particular scenario refers to events and objects within the scope of one's immediate vision. Characteristically, such language is both asyntactic and highly sensory. The implication of Verity's observation is that scenarios prepared for use at early stages of instruction should address the needs of the bioprogram. Although no substantive research has been done as yet on this subject, the line of reasoning is highly attractive. (For more on the bioprogram see Bickerton 1984.)

borsa are both nouns, do they belong to the same class or are there different classes of nouns in Italian?

The teacher should attempt to answer all student questions as directly as possible, without going into great detail (more on this point will be found in Chapter 5, "Debriefing"). The value of this approach lies in associating the conscious learning process as closely as possible with the awakening process of acquisition that is unconscious in each learner. Learners will not have the same concerns all at the same time (one of the reasons why the strategic interaction method does not accept the requirement of a strictly sequenced grammatical syllabus). Of course, the next step is to build on this good beginning. It is here that we rely on the group.

Language is generally a communal affair. Since people use it to communicate with others, the group has been integrated into the strategic interaction approach. The premise is that learners do not lose their creativity in language through the need to conform to those around them. Instead, each individual is seen as a contributing and cooperating member of a group, endowed with cognitive and affective powers to enable him or her to develop a personal competence in the new language while developing a new social presence. Groups in the interactive classroom have two major charges: (1) to create a script for a personal role in order to realize a given agenda and (2) to cooperate in the learning process. A particularly fitting definition of language in this view is offered by Edmonson (1981: 2): "Language is a means of doing things with words with people."

When working to fulfill its second charge, that is, conscious cooperating in the learning process, the group promotes a multiplier effect. When a member of the group needs to know about a specific matter regarding the target language, another member of the group may be able to supply an explanation that is both concise and to the point. Learning from peers is much less threatening under some circumstances than having a power figure, like the teacher, dictate an explanation. Moreover, the sharing of knowledge is increased when student peers contribute to the teaching process.

An analogous sharing of knowledge is not characteristic of the traditional foreign-language classroom. The traditional teacher retains the focus of attention, interacting singly with each student or with single groups. Students are rarely allowed to interact with each other, unless posed to do so in contrived situations by the teacher. The traditional network is depicted in Figure 2.1.

The strategic interaction classroom permits several patterns of interaction. By collaborating on the resolution of communicative problems, the teacher and the students find themselves shifting into a variety of interactive roles. At times, the teacher becomes a coach to the students

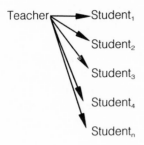

Figure 2.1   The traditional classroom network

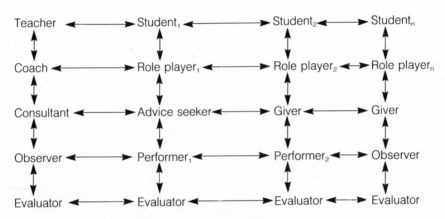

Figure 2.2   The strategic interaction classroom network

who are engaged in preparing their roles in the discourse. Students are alternately seekers and givers of information to their classmates. When the scenarios are performed, the teacher and the nonperforming members of the class turn into observers of those who are the active performers. Debriefing provides the opportunity for everyone to join in evaluating the performance. Figure 2.2 displays some of the interactive diversity in the strategic interaction classroom.

Going beyond the first day

On the days that follow the first one, the three phases of classroom activity – rehearsal, performance, and debriefing – should become distinct. Rehearsal and debriefing provide the opportunity to work on improving scenario performances. With its element of surprise or uncertainty, the performance phase continues to serve the function of motivating the students to fulfill their responsibilities in all three phases. As the purse-snatching episode illustrates, scenarios are mini-dramas that

21

happen because of an unexpected event or the need to resolve some dilemma of social interaction. In first-day scenarios, the rehearsal phase is combined with the performance phase, because the students have not yet acquired enough of the target language to work in small, independent groups. As the course continues, scenarios become more "personalized." Groups of students are provided with separate agendas to put into action. The agenda attached to each scenario role leads the group to map out a general game plan in anticipation of the performance phase (the details of writing scenarios are given in Chapter 3).

The three phases may vary considerably in length. As a general rule, it is wise to let each phase last as long as the students wish. Usually, the performance phase is the shortest of the three, especially at the outset of a course. Time of performance can range from a few minutes to over fifteen minutes. Rehearsals and debriefings tend to be longer; in fact, these phases may even stretch over more than one class period. It is the teacher's responsibility to observe students' behavior carefully and to terminate each phase when the students are ready to move on to the next one. (Chapters 4 and 5 provide discussions of what is expected in each of the three phases; see also the discussion of the basic steps in strategic interaction that follow).

The themes for scenarios can be taken from everyday life. For example, one group of students may be assigned the role of someone who has just purchased a defective item from a department store. Another group may be asked to play the part of the store representative who deals with complaints. During rehearsal, each group thinks over the options available for their role. For the customer:

1. get an exchange of the item for one that is not defective;
2. demand a refund of the money paid;
3. request that the item be repaired.

For the store representative:

1. convince the customer that the item is not defective and, if necessary, suggest that the item was in good working order when it left the store;
2. agree to exchange the item for another;
3. refund the customer's money;
4. offer to repair or adjust the item.

The differences in the priorities for each role will become apparent once the performance begins. Depending on the strategies used by each party, the two may decide on an option agreeable to both (an exchange, for example). On the other hand, they may not reach an agreement. This element of uncertainty is one of the strengths of the scenario, because it requires the interacting students to pay attention to what the other party is saying and to make adjustments in the game plan as the conversation continues. To assure that the element of uncertainty is maintained, it is essential that each role is prepared by different groups working separately from each other. No intergroup sharing of ideas is allowed until the debriefing that follows the performance, at which time the teacher might ask the assembled class to consider alternative solutions to the one taken.

The basic steps in strategic interaction

Once it has been decided that an interactive approach will be used predominantly or exclusively in the course, the teacher has seven tasks to complete:

(1) Review the coverage in the textbook. The purpose of this review is *not* to decide what points of grammar to address during the course of instruction. If the textbook is typical, all the basic grammar points will be there, in one form or another. The purpose of the review is to determine the subject matter of each unit, such as travel, lodging, shopping, eating in restaurants, socializing, attending school, and conducting business transactions.

(2) Prepare scenarios that relate to the subject areas as they are set forth in the text (or, alternatively, by the curriculum specialist). In this way, the textbook can be used by the students as a source of information about the target language while they prepare their roles in the scenarios.

(3) Look for reading selections that touch on the theme of the scenarios (see Chapter 7 for further discussion of this step).

(4) Be ready to play several types of instructional roles in the classroom. During rehearsals, the teacher will have to be a knower, a guide, a counselor, and a coach, as the students require various kinds of help. During performances, the teacher joins the audience as an observer but must also be ready to do some more coaching when needed. In the debriefing phase, the teacher takes on the roles of discussion leader and commentator (on the language used during the performance).

(5) Provide some writing exercises that derive from the scenarios (again, see Chapter 7 for more details).

(6) Prepare the outline for grammar logs to be used by the students for keeping a record of what they have learned about the language (see Chapter 5).

(7) Involve the students in the evaluation process. In a learner-centered approach to second-language instruction, evaluation should also be as learner-centered as possible. Students should be prepared to evaluate their own performances as well as those of their peers. The teacher should take these evaluations into consideration when making conclusions

about the achievement of each student. (More is said about evaluation in Chapter 8.)

Designing interactive curricula

Teachers as well as administrators tend to feel uneasy when faced with language courses devoid of syllabi. The curriculum is supposed to have objectives spelled out along with some detail about what is to be covered. From an interactive point of view, it seems irrelevant to develop semester plans based on structural points of grammar or even on functions and notions. Syllabi and curricula are by nature disjointed bodies. In a fully student-centered classroom, learning becomes a personal matter, with each student acquiring elements of the target language as they become meaningful. Teacher-originated schedules of grammatical and functional points cannot presume to dictate the acquisitional sequence for each student.

If syllabi are to serve as more than window dressing for the course of instruction, they should probably be based on some sequence of increasing interactive involvement in target-language discourse. To construct such syllabi requires that teachers look at real-life language use. What types of interactions are likely to require a minimum of verbalization? To lead students into authentic discourses in the target language, which scenarios should be placed first? Salah (1983) has already investigated the question of relative interactive complexity and language use. She concluded that some scenario themes are indeed simpler than others in terms of interaction and dependence on verbalization. Although the simple scenarios can be used at almost any time during the semester, complex ones cannot be used at the start. For example, requiring a nonsmoking student to converse with a heavy smoker who is violating the posted order *No Smoking* can evoke various attempts to communicate, from simple hand gestures to rather complex verbal requests not to smoke. Therefore, such a scenario can be used at any of several junctures during the semester. Other scenarios, such as the one in which a student must explain the reason for a failed exam, involve more complex interaction and require greater amounts of verbalizing in order to be played successfully. In laying out scenario themes for a semester, teachers may find it useful to think of their own experiences with interaction in the target-language community. Personal experiences can be a dependable guide to scenario sequencing in the absence of any developed framework. The next section will set forth some observations about scenarios and offer some guidelines.

Sequencing scenarios for a course of second-language instruction

The purpose of a scenario sequence is to involve learners in increasing degrees of interactive complexity while, at the same time, leading them through some predetermined schedule of matters to be learned in the target language. Ideally, the sequence takes learners from where they are when they begin the program of instruction (presumably at point zero) to where they can interact with others to fulfill all their communicative needs. The competence to interact in the target language must be achieved in all three dimensions of conversation (see Chapter 1) and not just in terms of how well learners manage to construct utterances. For each bit of information exchanged coherently, the appropriate control must be gained over strategies and counterstrategies.

The traditional inclination among teachers is to think in terms of grammatical progress. We are accustomed to worrying about how many words are being learned and how to teach the future tense or the modal auxiliaries. As the concern for expressing notions and performing functions spreads throughout the profession, many teachers react by adding these matters to the list of grammatical items in their syllabi. Perhaps it is too much to ask that yet another component be added to the list of things to be taught – namely the management of interactions. Actually, this proposal is more drastic than one might expect. I wish to suggest that a well-executed sequence of scenarios can serve as the main organizing principle of the subject matter. All other aspects (grammar, vocabulary, functions, and notions) can be introduced naturally as the scenarios are prepared, performed, and discussed throughout the semester. For the teacher who is not prepared to be so radical, any use of scenarios will be of benefit and can be introduced without significant disruption to the established routine.

Let us turn to the question of what features of scenarios should guide the sequencing arrangement. For ESL students (i.e., for students who are enrolled in English courses in a country where English is the main language), one should proceed in terms of relative degrees of urgency in communicative needs. When ESL students arrive in the United States, they immediately face problems of communication that require specific competences in English. These problems may disappear as students become adjusted, but other problems take their place. The question of relative difficulty in grammar and vocabulary is clearly not at issue here, since daily communicative needs must be met regardless of the contrived organization of a traditional syllabus. Actually, the case of the ESL student – or, for that matter, of anyone studying a new language in the country where it is spoken – can serve to inspire changes in all courses of second-language instruction.

The major task, then, is how to make scenarios reflect increasing levels of interactive difficulty. Investigations by Salah (1983) suggest that complexity in interaction grows at least in part from the amount of verbalization required to get through the scenario. Scenarios executed largely with gestures can be considered more elementary than those requiring extensive use of verbal language. It also appears that gesture-executed scenarios can be re-used at later stages in the course of instruction, at which times advancing students should be able to give them more verbal content and rely less on gestures. The more "difficult" scenarios (i.e., those requiring extensive verbalization in order to be performed) are not functional at early stages of instruction because they demand far more than the students can produce.

Puhl (1987) has worked out a sequence of twenty-two scenarios for ESL that is integrated with an independent exposition of grammatical elements. Scenario content was drawn from the perceived needs of the student body (in this case, adult ESL learners matriculating at a two-year college). In Puhl's approach, the teacher "models" preselected grammar points while explaining the scenario and while helping the students rehearse. These points become "target structures" available to the students as they perform their roles in the scenario. Topics for Puhl's scenarios include the following: what to do in the case of medical emergencies and accidents, how to deal with sales personnel when a purchased item turns out to be defective, and how to defend yourself if accused unjustly of theft or improper behavior on the job. The grammar point modeled for the first scenario was the present continuous tense. Puhl found that modeled structures occurred in spontaneous student talk in 75% of the cases. When structures were not modeled, they occurred in approximately 50% of the students' utterances. There was also some evidence that students transferred structures from one scenario to the next.

Puhl's approach requires teachers to impose constraints on their own use of structures and vocabulary. Not all teachers may be willing or able to do so. It may also be possible to sequence scenarios so that students are led from participation in collectivities to ultimate self-reliance as individuals acting alone. At least four levels of scenarios would mirror the emergence of individual second-language speakers from the matrix of the group:

LEVEL ONE

Learners are given membership in the group with no requirement to take individual stands in the discourse. The scenario presented earlier about the pickpocket on the bus is an illustration of a level-one scenario. While all participants react to the same event – the "theft" of a purse – each is free to engage in discourse or remain silent. The choice and extent of each student's intervention are unrestricted, but whatever is said contributes to the interest of the group as a reacting body.

LEVEL TWO

Participants act as members of a group, but diverse groups are required to interact with each other. Sham competitions can be set up between them; for example, one of the groups is given an unfair advantage so that it will win. The losing group is made aware of the unfair advantage. The discussion that takes place between the winners and the losers constitutes the actual performance phase of the scenario. Later, the teacher should admit to the set-up and reward each team equally. (See "The Contest," p. 53, for a full description of this scenario.)

LEVEL THREE

Participants are called upon to play independent roles, but these roles are strongly marked by social conventions. A scenario concerning a mislaid bus transfer might be a good example for this level: Both the passenger and the bus driver are caught up in the urgency of the situation. The bus driver cannot take much time with passengers who lose transfers, even though the passenger may need to arrive at some destination as quickly as possible but does not have enough money for a taxi.

LEVEL FOUR

Learners participate in actions not predominantly influenced by social conventions. Scenarios at this level tend to address situations relating to home life or the workplace. An individual may be offered a promotion that would take him or her away from an infirm and widowed parent. The parent may have his or her own agenda, such as remarriage. The ensuing exchange between the two allows them to project personal opinions and attitudes about important social matters.

Deriving scenarios from noninteractive text materials

Teachers wishing to use scenarios but constrained to follow preselected textbooks may look to these very materials for scenario themes. For example, one college-level elementary German textbook gives the following as an exercise in a lesson on shopping:

> You have just returned from Germany. Describe some shopping customs you observed there.

27

At best, such an exercise would yield a brief paragraph of declarative sentences repeating or paraphrasing the sample utterances given in the dialog of the unit. It can be turned into a lively two-role scenario by creating a situation that might involve an English-speaking American trying to be a shopper in a German setting. Since part of the lexical content of the theme of this particular unit involved the purchase of flowers, the following scenario was found to be appropriate:

Scenario Title: Try Saying It with Flowers

Role A: (male or female) You run a flower shop. You have fresh roses but your other flowers are not fresh (they are wilted). If you don't sell them soon, you will have to destroy them or throw them away. As a result, you will lose money. Try to sell the old flowers to the next customer.

Role B: (male) You have just met a young German woman. She has invited you to dinner. You have been told that you should bring flowers to your hostess. Roses are especially fitting in these situations. Prepare yourself to purchase some flowers in the flower shop.

The two roles can also be given in German:

Titel: Sag es mit Blumen

Rolle A: Sie besitzen einen Blumenladen. Sie haben frische Rosen, aber die anderen Blumen sind nicht frisch (sie sind welk). Wenn Sie sie nicht bald verkaufen, müsen Sie sie zerstören, oder wegwerfen. Sie verlieren damit Geld. Versuchen Sie, dem Einkäufer die alten Blumen zu verkaufen.

Rolle B: Sie haben vor kurzem eine junge Dame kennengelernt. Sie hat Sie zum Abendessen eingeladen. Man hat Ihnen gesagt, dass man bei Einladungen der Dame des Hauses Blumen bringt. Die Rosen sind die Blumen, die man bei dieser Art von Gelegenheit bringen soll. Wie stellen Sie sich an, in einem Laden Blumen zu kaufen?

Since the classroom teacher in this instance was not experienced with the strategic interaction approach, the following suggestions were offered to the teacher to help him guide each group as they rehearsed their roles:

> *Suggestions for Role A*: You could tell the customer that the carnations (or some other flowers) are somewhat old and so are being sold at a special, low price. If the customer insists on fresher flowers, you might lower the price even more.
> You could also ask the customer what the occasion is for the flowers. Depending on his answer, you might try to convince him that some other flower would be more appropriate than the fresh roses.

Suggestions for Role B: If the salesperson tries to sell you some flowers other than the ones you want to buy, you might either insist on the roses or strike a bargain about the other flowers. Perhaps you can buy some of each.

Suggestions for both roles: Be sure you know the names of various kinds of flowers. You should also know how to say "fresh," "old," and "wilted," together with the comparative construction in German.

As it turned out in actual performances of this scenario, students used grammatical structures that had been presented formally in the unit from which the scenario had been derived. They also used some structures that had not been presented previously, such as the dependent clause in the following sentence:

Haben Sie keine Blumen, *die frisch sind*?
('Don't you have any flowers *that are fresh?*')

The first attempt to produce this utterance yielded an error of word order. The teacher quickly gave the correct form and the student continued speaking. Among the grammar points explicitly presented in the unit were the negative article (*kein*) and the proper affirmative response to a question that is posed in the negative (*Haben Sie keine Blumen ... ?*). Students made errors on both counts, saying *nicht eine* for *keine* and responding *Ja* for *Doch*. Although no direct transfer was noted from the formal exercises on these grammar points to their use in conversation, students became aware of their significance, and instances of error diminished through the performances of the scenario.

The teacher expressed concern that the students were trying to use a dependent clause before it had been formally introduced, but the students experienced no greater difficulty in using it than they did with the grammar points that had been presented. Although no students asked for an explanation of the dependent clause after the performance, the teacher felt obliged to give one, anyway – a practice not without question. In view of the foregoing, the following advice is given to the teacher who wishes to derive scenarios from currently used text materials: Expect your students to use grammar that has not been formally introduced. Use your own discretion in explaining matters not included in the unit being studied. If students ask for an explanation, give it to them, by all means. Otherwise, the proper target-language form may be all that is necessary.

To provide further illustrations of how scenarios can be derived from noninteractive materials, the following were constructed for English-speaking American students of Spanish published in 1984 by Heinle and Heinle of Boston:

Título del escenario: ¡Alarma!

Papel A: Estás paseando por la calle y ves que está saliendo mucho humo de la ventana del segundo piso de la casa de tu novio/a. Vas a la puerta y llamas, pero nadie contesta. Sin embargo, en la esquina hay un teléfono especial para llamar a los bomberos. Prepárate para hacer la llamada telefónica necesaria.

Papel B: Eres coordinador de una estación de bomberos. Tu jefe te informó que los bomberos han recibido muchas llamadas falsas. Hay que tener cuidado con las llamadas falsas. En este momento recibes una llamada de emergencia. ¿Qué vas a preguntar para averiguar si es o no es una llamada falsa?

Scenario Title: Alarm!

Role A: You are walking down the street and you notice that a lot of smoke is coming out of the window on the second floor of your boy/girlfriend's house. You go to the door and knock, but nobody answers. However, there is a special telephone at the corner of the street, to call the fire station. Prepare yourself to make the necessary telephone call.

Role B: You are the coordinator at a fire station. Your chief has informed you that the fire station has received many false alarms. You have to be careful about such alarms. Just now, you receive an emergency call. What are you going to ask in order to determine if it is another false alarm?

This scenario was based on a unit dealing with fire fighters and vocabulary associated with fire stations. As in all scenarios involving interaction among students, the roles are written on separate slips of paper and distributed to different groups of students. No group is allowed to know the contents of the agenda given to the other group.

The following scenario is from a unit dealing with the bakery and baked goods.

Título del escenario: ¿Seguro que no voy a engordar?	*Scenario Title*: Are You Sure I Won't Gain Weight?
Papel A: Eres el proprietario de una panadería. Una especialidad tuya es los dulces de pocas calorías. Pero todos se han vendido yá. Quedan sólo los otros dulces que engordan. Viene alguien para comprar dulces. Prepárate para venderle estos dulces.	*Role A*: You are the owner of a bakery. One of your specialties is low-calorie sweets. Unfortunately, you've sold your entire supply for the day. The only remaining sweets are the fattening ones. Someone comes to buy sweets. Prepare yourself to sell the ones you have.
Papel B: El médico te puso a una dieta muy rigurosa. No puedes comer dulces que llevan muchas calorías. Lees en el periódico un anuncio de una panadería donde se venden dulces hechos con azucar sintética que no tiene muchas calorías. Tienes gana de comer algo dulce pero con muy pocas calorías. ¿Qué le preguntas al panadero para estar seguro/a que estos dulces no engordan?	*Role B*: The doctor has put you on a strict diet. You must not eat high-calorie desserts. You have seen an ad in the paper about a bakery where low-calorie sweets are sold. You would like to eat something sweet but not with a lot of calories. What will you ask the baker to be certain that the advertised sweets are not fattening?

Strategies

It should be obvious by now that all scenarios require strategies. Not only are the participants required to anticipate what strategies they will use while engaged in rehearsal, they will probably also have to make adjustments as the situation changes during the performance of the scenario. Strategies vary considerably from speaker to speaker, as well as from language to language, and therein lies the problem of discussing them as absolutes. They also change with the times. In the 1950s, a common "pick-up" strategy used at social gatherings in the United States was the question, "Say, haven't we met somewhere before?" The strategic value of this utterance might not be carried over to another language even when its form is similar in that language. For example, one German equivalent does not come out as a question: *Ich glaube, wir kennen uns* (literally, 'I think we know each other'). If a German learner of English were to attempt this strategy in a literal translation from German, the English-speaking person to whom the strategy was directed might take it as a forthright question rather than an overture to become better acquainted. (During the 1970s and 1980s, the form of this strategy was altered and was expressed as a question one might ask about the other's astrological sign.)

It is not necessary for the teacher to lay out a detailed schema for strategies. It is sufficient to be aware of the wide range of potential strategies likely to be implemented by students. The illustrations that follow are intended as a guide to teachers who wish to become more aware of the diverse types of strategies found in natural discourse. Since the strategies are taken from English as spoken in North America, there may not be exact equivalents among persons speaking other languages.

DISCLAIMERS

At times, we find it useful or even necessary to give criticism. Since such an activity may draw the other's fire in return, we can decide to use a "disclaimer." We may feign clumsiness or inability to make the criticism, as in "I don't know how to tell you this, but ... " Another ploy might be to state one's own displeasure at giving the news ("I hate to be the one to tell you this, but ... "). Yet another possible technique is to ask the person's permission to make the criticism beforehand ("Do you mind if I make a personal remark?").

POSTSCRIPTS

Special requests sometimes come as "postscripts" to a conversation. In this way, the requester plays down the significance of the request. Postscripts are introduced by expressions like "By the way ... ," "While we're on the subject ... ," and "Incidentally ... ."

APOLOGIES

Some people, even when they will accept responsibility for a transgression, try to save as much "face" as possible in making their apologies. Being on the losing end of one interaction is sometimes unavoidable, but the transgressor can always look forward to being right another time. Some apologies in English can take the following forms:

"I'm really sorry for what happened. I'm sure you'd understand if you had been in my shoes."
"Yes, I was responsible for the accident, but the surface of the road was very icy."

"I really don't deserve it, but I hope you will find it in your heart to forgive me."

THE ONEUP

It sometimes happens that one person can force the other to acknowledge an interactive victory. To verbalize the advantage gained enhances one's position in future interactions. "One-ups" are usually brief and cutting: "I told you so." "Didn't I tell you?" "What did I say?"

Strategies often stand in contrasting pairs. In other words, for many strategies there are counterstrategies. Consider the following dialog in which an apology is followed by a one-up:

A: I'm really sorry.
B: Didn't I tell you that would happen?

A can terminate the dialog at this point or go on to repeat the apology, rephrase it, or acknowledge B's superior position, saying something like: "You were right, after all." If B persists in expressing a superior position, A might remind B that the apology was made as it should have been: "Well, I *said* I was sorry! What more do you want?"

REFUSALS

There are many ways to refuse offers or overtures. The choice of expression depends on the relative status of the speakers and the implications of the refusal for future interactions. Freundlich (1981) describes several forms refusals can take, as in the following exchanges:

A: Care to see a movie?
B: There's a program on TV I want to watch.

(The refusal is veiled as a statement of prior commitment.)

A: Have some rattlesnake meat.
B: Thanks, but my doctor tells me to avoid eating reptile.

(The refusal comes out as an unquestionable statement of authority.)

B: I forgot to tell you that I'm a vegetarian.

(The refusal is couched as a statement of religious or ethical conviction and therefore is unassailable by a gracious host.)

33

DEFENSIVE STRATEGIES

In the heat of an interchange, a verbal attack is sometimes mounted which erodes one's position so greatly that a defensive posture must be assumed. One effective defensive strategy is to change to a topic on which a new offensive can be mounted (see Rumelhart 1983). A topic change may be attempted in many ways. One may simply ask permission: "Do you mind if we talk about something else?" Alternatively, one might just start talking about another matter and hope to use the expressions "by the way" or "incidentally" to initiate a topic change (note that these expressions also are used to express a postscript).

Use of the topic-change strategy can be conditioned by the relative level of prestige or power of those involved in the interaction. A student being scolded by the teacher for giving a poor performance on a test is rarely able to change the topic of the discourse. Neither would a speeder who has been detained by a police officer and is being reprimanded. As a general rule, change of topic is less restricted when the speakers belong to the same peer group.

Learning and communicating strategies

The literature on second language acquisition reveals a growing interest among methodologists and researchers in what are called *learning strategies*. Grouped under this heading are the routines used by learners in order to gain competence in the target language. Rubin and Thompson (1982) discuss some effective learning strategies observed among students enrolled in second-language courses.

Communicating strategies comprise those ploys used by nonnatives who are struggling to make themselves understood by speakers of the target language (see, for example, Faerch and Kasper 1983). The strategies occurring in natural discourse, discussed in the previous sections of this chapter, differ from learning or communicating strategies in that they are used in situations where the learning of a new code and the clarification of an information exchange are not at issue. Nevertheless, teachers would do well to promote the implementation of communicating strategies by their students and even to facilitate their conversations by providing them with target-language expressions like the following: "Sorry, I didn't understand. Please repeat." or "Could you say that again?" Expressions like "Just a moment, please." and "How do you say that in X?" are useful when interacting students interrupt their conversations in order to ask members of their respective groups for special help. (See Labarca and Khanji 1986 for an investigation into the effect of strategy interaction on students' use of communication strategies.)

Protocols

The term "protocol" is used here to label a class of routines that are similar to strategies insofar as they relate to the manipulation of language beyond its use to convey information. Protocols are different from strategies in that their use is dictated more by cultural convention than by the intentions of those involved in the interaction. A common protocol is the salutation used by people when they encounter each other, such as "Hello," "Hi," *Ciao*, *¡Hóla!*. Another example can be found in what people are expected to say when they bump into someone in a crowded place. In fact, we can even go so far as to "grade" bumping protocols in terms of how serious the bump was:

Least Serious   "Oops!"
                "Sorry..."
                "I'm *so* sorry."
Most Serious   "My God! Did I hurt you?"

Protocols lend themselves to classification according to their general social uses, as in the following examples:

1. *Moving in traffic.*
   Requesting permission to occupy a space ("Is this seat taken?").
   Passing someone ("Excuse me, can I get by?").
   Bumping ("Sorry," "Excuse me," etc.).
   The teacher of Spanish or Italian will notice that these languages have a special protocol (Spanish: *con permiso*, Italian: *con permesso*) that can be used to pass someone or occupy a space but not as an excuse for bumping. As a result, it covers only part of the interactive terrain of the English "Excuse me" protocol. An English-speaking student of Spanish must learn to say *con permiso* upon entering a crowded elevator rather than *¡Perdón!* if the expectation is that people will move aside without being jostled.
2. *Rites of passage* (Erving Goffman's term for the linguistic and social marking of changes in status).
   Marriage ("Congratulations," "Best Wishes").
   Anniversaries ("Happy Birthday").
   Death ("I'm sorry," "You have my condolences").
3. *Holidays.*
   "Merry Christmas."

"Happy New Year." etc.

In American English, probably the only time people use the word "merry" in a greeting is on the occasion of Christmas. Such fossilization of linguistic forms is a characteristic of protocols, especially when they are more usually written than spoken. Sometimes the fossilization is so extensive that the component parts of a protocol lose their individuality as words, as in the expression "Goodbye," which developed from an original four-word phrase: "God be with you." Of course, the immediately important point for the learner is that speakers of the target language are not likely to reflect on the history of protocols but will expect to use them or hear them used in their customary contexts.

4. *Daily functions.*

Attending a party ("Welcome," "Glad you could come").

Leaving a party ("Must you go so soon?" from the host and "I really enjoyed it" from a guest).

Eating meals ("Please begin," "Enjoy it").

American English does not have an exact counterpart to the French *Bon appétit* with which to start a meal, but it does have expressions like "Help yourself" that can be used during mealtime. Depending on the level of formality of the meal, there may be a host who begins and ends the ritual in some marked way. For example, to signal the impending end of a formal repast, the host might say, "Let's go into the other room and have some dessert." This lets the guests know that there will be no more courses served at the table. The offering of toasts during a formal meal is also subjected to protocols in many cultures. In some cultures, no one drinks from his or her glass until the host (or an honored guest) proposes a toast.

5. *Conversational management.*

A considerable amount of work has been done recently on how people manage the flow of conversation (see, for example, Tannen 1984). Although the term "protocol" has not been applied to the various devices used, they fit the definition and can be classified here:

Beginning a conversation:

with a stranger ("Excuse me, but...," "Hello there...")

with an acquaintance ("Hi! How are you today?")

with a close friend   ("What's up?" "What's happening?")

Showing attentiveness during a monolog:

"Yes, yes..."

"Uh-huh..."

"Yeah..."

"Really?" (*with animation*)

Signal to bring about a closing:

"I'll talk to you later, if I can."
"Sorry, but I've got to go now."

The study of protocols leads to a close investigation of the culture that accompanies the language to be learned. The foregoing examples are given to suggest the significance of protocols for the basic activities of life. Ignoring or avoiding them can make the violator seem ill-mannered or ignorant. Of course, learners enjoy a special status as nonnatives and may not be held to the same requirements to use the proper protocols. But it is preferable instead to gain cultural competence. See Brown (1985) for how to employ strategic interaction in teaching telephone protocols in Spanish.

Nonverbals

Gestures

The significance of nonverbal elements must not be downplayed in an interactive approach to second-language instruction. Nonverbals, such as hand gestures and body posturing, do more than embellish the verbal content of the discourse. They are often an integral part of it. The following informal introduction cannot be executed in English without a hand gesture by the person doing the introducing (Mary, in this case):

Mary: Joe, Bill. Bill, Joe.
Joe: Hi, Bill.
Bill: Hi, Joe.

The handshake by Joe and Bill is, of course, an optional nonverbal. If we change the setting to a more formal one, the handshake becomes obligatory and the introducer may replace her hand gesture with a turning of her head in the direction of each person as she names him:

Mary: Mr. Smith, Mr. Jones. Mr. Jones, Mr. Smith.
Mr. Smith: How do you do?
Mr. Jones: Hello!

Although the achievement of skills in the target language is measured most appropriately in terms of the verbal component, we must not let our students disregard the need to acquire the proper nonverbals along the way.

Intonation

Intonation is another matter of significance in learning a new language. Unfortunately, textbook illustrations of intonation usually consist of sentences given out of context. The rise and fall of tones and the change in levels of stress are likely to be illustrated primarily as they accompany interrogative and declarative sentences. Extending intonation beyond this limit is difficult unless it is associated with the strategic intent of the speaker and is treated as an integral part of connected discourse. Take, for example, the sentence "Where did you get that dress?" How is this sentence to be performed? Is it to be delivered as a request for factual information? If so, the voice is likely to start at a low pitch and stay there until the final word is reached, at which point it would rise and fall abruptly (in American English, of course). But what if the sentence is to be delivered in shock or disbelief that anyone would dare to wear such a dress? Then the voice would have to fluctuate up and down, perhaps with a loud stress on "that," as in "Where did you get *that* dress!"

Laughter

Laughter also carries strategic functions. First of all, there is the nervous laughter of students as they gather to rehearse or perform in scenarios. The laughter of students observing their classmates in performance may not reflect normal audience behavior but may be triggered by feelings of solidarity or acceptance of what is being said in the scenario. Outside the learning context, laughter may serve a wide number of functions. It is sometimes a "parenthesizer" to enforce a verbal strategy, as in "By the way (*heh, heh*), I want you to know...". It can mean disbelief (as in the solitary laugh *ha!*) or discovery (*Ha, há!*) or even heartiness (*Ho, ho, ho!*).

Functions and notions

The functional-notional syllabus of the Council of Europe (see, for example, Wilkins 1976 and van Ek 1975) represented a major effort to break with the practice inherited from early audiolingualism to concentrate on form in foreign-language instruction. The intent of those who proposed the functional-notional syllabus was to identify essential concepts and purposes of communication so that the learner could be guided in acquiring communicative competence in the target language. Included under the heading of notions are such concepts as time, quantity, and space. Functions are subdivided into judging and evaluating, "suasion" (persuading, commanding, etc.), arguing, making rational inquiries, expressing personal emotions, and affirming emotional relations (greetings, gratitude, flattery). It was assumed that all learners − at least those involved with European languages − would need to find expression for such notions and functions in the target language.

There are two major problems with the functional-notional syllabus. First, no suggestion is given as to how such a syllabus fits into any particular teaching approach. As a free-standing list, it is no more pedagogically suggestive than a syllabus of grammatical elements or a word list would be. Second, the functional-notional syllabus mixes philosophical concepts with potential strategies and protocols and does not relate them to conversational game plans. The transactional value of any utterance must be interpreted in the context of a particular speaker working through a scenario with a personal game plan in mind. Personal game plans, as described earlier in this chapter, are necessary if students are to implement strategies in meaningful ways. Participants in conversations must be prepared to adjust the strategies of their game plans as the intentions of others become evident to them. A language function becomes a strategy only when it is used in the execution of a game plan.

Whether we like it or not, human interactions are by nature risky. Every time we speak to other people we expose our self-esteem to possible criticism. The goals we wish to attain must be approached through negotiating. Mistakes made along the way cause us to suffer considerable psychological anguish. We cannot afford to be philosophical about our task. In learning to speak a new language we must become as familiar as possible with the protocols its speakers use. We must also strive to find the proper expression of the personal strategies we wish to execute.

Target- and native-language use in strategic interaction

The belief remains strong that the target language should be used as much as possible right from the first day. Such a practice supposedly forces students to "think" in the target language. However, the breakdown in communication caused by this narrow view of language use may outweigh any benefit.

Certainly, use of the native language facilitates the making of explanations and the setting up of various exercises. In the strategic interaction approach, a further articulation is made of the use of the target and native languages in the classroom. Basically, strategic interaction values *intensity* of target-language use over frequency. Intensity is here defined to mean self-generated discourse in interaction with others. Thus, the short, intense interactions of even simple scenarios are highly significant when they are executed in the target language. When the strategic interaction approach is working as it should, interactions in the target language increase in length and complexity throughout the semester. Eventually, the target language may even take over the functions of rehearsal and debriefing as the students become more comfortable in it.

As the course of instruction goes on from day to day, the teacher and the learners become increasingly aware of individual differences in interactive style. As Littlewood observes, the most efficient communicators in the class are not necessarily those who best manipulate structures or command large vocabularies. Efficient communicators in the classroom, as in real life, are people who appraise the nature of the speech situation, take account of shared information, and then select the strategies that are most effective (Littlewood 1984: 4). Being "talkative" is not always the mark of an effective communicator. Each student must find the measure of language use that is personally best suited. Participation in scenario rehearsal, as well as in debriefing, may be the most that some students are willing to undertake. With time, these same students may feel more at ease performing for an audience – but such a demand must not be made a necessary condition for evaluation in the course of instruction.

Summary

The starting point for an interactive approach to second-language instruction is getting the students to generate their own discourse. The motivational value of self-generated discourse for students is evident when compared to discourse that is contrived by the teacher. The key device to use in promoting student-generated discourse is the scenario as executed in the sequence of rehearsal, performance, and debriefing. However, since absolute beginners do not have sufficient knowledge of the target language to engage in rehearsals, early (i.e., "first-day") scenarios are set up to combine rehearsal with performance. In doing so, the teacher acts as a giver of information and supplies the students with target-language equivalents to what they wish to say as they react to the situations in which they find themselves. As instruction progresses, rehearsal emerges as a distinct phase during which students prepare game plans. An important task for the teacher is to find or create scenarios that take the students into ever deepening levels of involvement with the target language. The sequence of scenarios in a course of instruction may be linked to an independent grammatical syllabus but should not be guided mainly by such a syllabus. The most important element in arranging scenarios is their relative interactive complexity. Scenarios may also be derived from standard, noninteractive lessons in a textbook. It is preferable, however, to view the textbook as an adjunct to the execution of scenarios.

The performing of scenarios involves the interplay of verbal strategies. All speakers use strategies in order to achieve their ends in discourse. These strategies can be classified according to the function they play in conversation (e.g., making apologies, giving disclaimers). Some strategies are ritualized (protocols). In addition, second-language students will need to resort to learning and communicating strategies.

3 The scenario

The scenario lies at the heart of the strategic interaction approach. Through it, students are led to create discourse in the target language that embodies the drama of real life.[1] The dramatic essence of the scenario was highlighted in the preface and the first chapter, where it was described as a realistic happening involving the unexpected and requiring the use of language to be resolved. We are ready now for a more precise definition:

> A scenario is a strategic interplay of roles functioning to fulfill personal agendas within a shared context.

This formal definition of the scenario conveniently sets forth its essential features: strategic interplay, roles, personal agendas, and shared context. Once we have some understanding of each feature, we will proceed to illustrations of various types of scenarios. A sample scenario as actually rehearsed, performed, and debriefed is given in Chapter 8.

Elements of the scenario

Strategic interplay

We humans interact with each other in a number of different ways. In some instances, our interactions are nothing more than the playing out of social conventions in which we come to rely heavily on protocols. The verbal content of such interactions is so fully predictable that we hardly pay attention to what the other party is saying, for example:

A: Hi there!
B: Hi! What's new?
A: Not much. On my way to work.
B: OK. See you later.

---

1 A recent study in first language acquisition adds support to the notion that dramatic activities contribute significantly to learning. Pellegrini (1984) finds that children who were allowed to engage in dramatic play on given topics were more able to lexicalize meanings on those same topics than children who were limited to discussing the topics or drawing pictures about them.

41

Although students should learn such protocols as "What's new?" and "See you later," the interplays dominated by them are not very conducive to scenario use. The interplays in a scenario should not be automatic. They should lead the participants to listen with more than a passing interest to what the other is saying. Ideally, there should be some ambiguity as to each party's motives. Some effort should be required of each before choosing what to say next. An exchange such as the following would indicate that the persons involved in it are not simply paying lip service to social conventions:

A: Got a minute?
B: Not really. I'm in a hurry.
A: It's about my job.
B: Let me finish my evaluation before we talk.
A: I've had some new expenses lately.
B: I'm sure that we'll find something else for you.
A: But I'm talking about my salary!

We can imagine that A is an employee who wants a raise and B, an employer who may be thinking of giving A a demotion. One indication of A's intentions can be found in the line "I've had some new expenses lately." B's rejoinder ("I'm sure that we'll find something else for you") reveals a very different view of the situation. Some ambiguity lingers, however, since B may be talking about a better position for A. Whatever the case, the conversation between the two is more than just an exchange of factual information. Each line has a strategic value that will lead – it is hoped – to an end desired by the parties involved. Since the two do not have the same agenda, the end is not likely to please both. As often happens in real life, the conversation may be cut off abruptly, with neither party being satisfied or with one party prevailing over the other. Of course, A and B are fictitious and so is their conversation. But if you or I were actually cast in similar roles, we would feel firsthand the drama of the scene. We might not create a conversation precisely like this one, but we would choose what to say with care because of our stake in the outcome. We would not be playing out a social ritual. The strategic value of our utterances would depend on our skills as communicators. In the case of the second-language learner, a third factor comes into play, namely competence in the target language and the mechanisms of conversational management that pertain to the target language. It is as a means to achieving this competence that the scenario exchange must be strategic in nature.

Roles

The next important element in our definition of the scenario is the roles as played by those involved in the discourse. We make ourselves known to others just as others make themselves known to us – primarily through verbal encounters. A stranger who stops us in the street to ask about the time cannot be known to us beyond this fleeting moment and the terse verbal activity of our meeting. In most cultures of the world, people are expected to be polite to strangers who follow accepted protocols when they speak. We can be no more than polite with strangers because there is no time to build much of anything else in the relationship. It is not by chance that the beginning chapters of many foreign-language textbooks are characterized by dialogs between strangers. Teaching students how to be polite with strangers is considered to be easier than involving them in strategic exchanges right from the start. As we pointed out in Chapter 2 in connection with the discourse generated by the pickpocket scenario, such is not necessarily the case. In fact, what is easy is not to be equated with what is useful or realistic in the classroom setting. Knowing how to ask directions is useless if the person addressed is unwilling to play the role of information supplier.

Through repeated encounters with other people, we begin to create a definable self in the target language. People get to know us by becoming the recipients of the verbal and nonverbal reactions we give in an array of episodes. Perhaps no response is needed to someone who is unwilling to play the role that is complementary to ours. Yet we should at least be able to understand the expression of that unwillingness. If second-language instruction is to promote communicative competence, then teachers must face the obligation to help students understand the roles of others and find the language that is appropriate to play them. Roles range from the socially constrained ones that can be defined by describing a set of circumstances (e.g., you are a tourist whose baggage has been lost) to the psychological roles we all play independently of circumstance (e.g., "friend," "confidant," "rival").

Many language teachers are already familiar with role plays and use them regularly in their classrooms. Savignon (1983: 209–10) cites some examples:

1. You are in the post office to mail a letter. Ask for the rates.
2. Make an apology to a passerby whose packages you have knocked to the ground.
3. You have been invited to dine in a restaurant. Order a meal that will not exceed your host's budget.

Standard role plays can often be enhanced into scenario roles by pairing them with another role so that an interaction can take place. For example, the role plays in the foregoing list can be expanded as follows:

43

Strategic interaction

1. At the post office (role pair: customer/clerk)

Role A: The letter you are to mail must arrive safely but not necessarily in a hurry. Prepare to ask the postal clerk about the rates and then decide which rate would be appropriate for your letter.

Role B: You are a postal clerk trying to service a crowd of people who are mailing their tax reports at the last moment. Here comes a customer with questions about postal rates. Prepare yourself to handle his or her questions expeditiously.

2. Shopping (role pair: accident perpetrator/victim)

Role A: You are trying to catch a bus and you inadvertently run into a passerby loaded down with packages. What will you say to this person? Remember that the bus is about to leave.

Role B: You have just bought some delicate china and someone has bumped into you, knocking your package to the ground. What will you say to this person?

3. Dining out (role pair: guest/host)

Role A: You are the guest at a business dinner. Your host represents a firm with which your company is trying to establish a relationship. This firm has a reputation for lavish entertaining. You must decide on a meal from the menu. What price meal will you select?

Role B: You are entertaining someone at a business dinner. Your boss has told you to cut back somewhat on expenses but not to be obvious about it to your guest. How will you react to your guest's choice of a meal?

Since pairing is an important feature of roles in the classroom as well as in real life, we need to discuss it in greater detail. First, however, there are some general observations to make about the role concept.

Roles are not easy to define in absolute terms. One thing about them is certain: They are neither static nor invariable. Rather, they are patterns of behavior. They are not always played well or uniformly. Every waiter in every restaurant in the world has a personal way of playing that role beyond the cultural and socioeconomic constraints placed upon it. Every mother has a way of talking to her children that reflects her parental role without having always to say the equivalent of "Remember, I'm your mother..."

What is even more complicated about roles is that they appear to be of two major but overlapping types. For simplicity's sake, let us use the labels "psychological" and "social" to identify them. Psychological roles include those established by Berne (1972) as "adult," "parent," and "child," as well as others such as "friend," "enemy," "rival," "lover." Social roles grow from societal functions, such as "vendor," "buyer," "teacher," "police officer," "tourist," and "client." Some social roles are marked as such by location, activity, and/or manner of dress. In the case of such marking, we can say that the roles are *overt*. Every society has keepers of the public peace and performers of community services that it places in uniforms and calls police, postal workers, tourist guides, and so on. Department stores often require that their staff wear special clothing or pins to distinguish them as salespersons. There are also *covert* roles in society. Most, if not all, of the psychological roles would not be marked in any outward way and so would have to be classified as covert ones. Some roles vary from overt to covert, such as undercover department store police, church authorities who may or may not wear ecclesiastical garb, and university professors who do not dress in their academic robes throughout the year.

Although we cannot play all possible roles all the time in our daily lives, we are likely to be called upon to play several roles from the social and psychological groups at the same time. One can easily imagine, for example, an automobile salesman who has his father as a customer, or a doctor who is treating her mother for a serious illness.

As mentioned earlier, an important feature of roles is that they are paired. In pairing, roles are set up so that the speakers share a reason for interacting with each other but do not necessarily have the same goal. When the paired roles are cast so that their cooperation is of mutual benefit to them – that is, each needs the other to realize its full potential – we say that they are complementary role pairs. Some examples of complementary pairs would be donor/recipient, host/guest, and employer/employee. Since doctors need patients in order to fulfill their medical role and patients need doctors in order to be treated, the doctor/patient role pair is also complementary. Of course, in the happy classroom where everything runs smoothly, teachers and students are in complementation. Many other illustrations can be found in public interactions where the roles are clearly marked and the goals shared, such as in the pair information seeker/information giver. Often, the conversation that results from such interactions has a low degree of strategic interplay:

A: Can you tell me where the station is?
B: Straight ahead, two miles.
A: Thank you.

When two roles come together that are not working toward achievement of a common goal, such as salesperson/window-shopper, we say that the pair is noncomplementary. Noncomplementary pairs produce conversations that have a greater degree of strategic interplay, because each will try to lead the other into playing a role that would be complementary:

A: May I help you?
B: Just looking.
A: Have you seen our new sweaters?
B: I really don't need any sweaters, thanks.
A: They're on sale.
B: Thank you, but I'd rather just browse by myself for a while.

Haggling provides another example of noncomplementary roles that lead to strategic interplay. It is a necessity in many countries where playing the vendor's role is a matter of day-by-day survival. The following is a conversation reported by a student who lived in South America and did her marketing almost daily:

Woman: (*showing mild interest in some fruit*) ¿Cuánto cuestan?

Woman: How much do they cost?

Vendor: A treinta la mano.

Vendor: Thirty a bunch.

Woman: Están muy caros. (*starts to walk away*)

Woman: They're very expensive.

Vendor: Señora, venga. (*gestures for her to return*)

Vendor: Please come back, ma'am.

Woman: (*says nothing but turns to come back*)

Vendor: Porque es Usted, se los doy a veinte.

Vendor: Just for you, I'll let them go for twenty.

Woman: No. Yo sé que sólo valen diez. No le doy ní un centavo más. (*begins to walk away again*)

Woman: No. I know that they're worth only ten. I won't give you a centavo more.

Vendor: Señora, venga. Soy muy pobre, tengo muchos hijos. Como Usted sabe, la vida es muy cara. ¡Ande, déme los veinte centavos!

Vendor: Please don't go away, Ma'am. I'm very poor. I've got a large family. You know that it is expensive to live these days. Come, now! Please give me the twenty centavos!

Woman: (*showing her hand as a potential customer*) No, le doy sólo diez. Mire, si le compro dos manos ¿me las da a 22 centavos?

Woman: No, I'm giving you only ten. Look, if I buy two bunches, will you sell them to me for 22 centavos?

Vendor: ¡Déme 25 por dos!	Vendor: Give me 25 centavos for two bunches.
Woman: Está bien. *(finally converting her role into that of a customer)*	Woman: All right.

There is much to say about the effect that speaking a new language has on students. Some students use the target language as a vehicle for "fantasy trips." One female Spanish speaker felt that English gave her a sense of freedom to discuss topics that would not be part of her discoursive range in Spanish. An English-speaking student appeared to lose his timidity and become aggressive when playing out roles in French. Although these students are probably catering to stereotypes, their behavior does reflect a willingness to enter into interaction with speakers of the target language. With time, students should be able to establish well-balanced roles in the target language.

The playing of long-term roles brings special difficulty in the context of formal second-language instruction. By "long-term" is meant the type of role that continues over several interactive episodes. The "rival" is an example of such a role. In order to play it successfully, one needs the memory of past encounters with one's opposite. These encounters lead the rival to use address forms, strategies, and nonverbal elements in ways that may not come out in only one detached encounter. "Competitor," on the other hand, is a short-term role, since it can be contained within one episode involving a contest of some sort. Not surprisingly, textbooks are likely to concentrate on treating short-term roles more frequently, since each chapter or unit introduces new and distinct matters. The "open-ended" scenario, discussed later in this chapter, is a way to accommodate long-term roles in a course of instruction.

Personal agendas and shared contexts

Each party in a scenario must be given an agenda that requires interaction with other parties in order to be completed. The best agendas are those that rest on a base of shared information and perhaps even interests – a shared context – but have different goals. Students should not be assigned agendas that impose value judgments or prejudge outcomes. The following are two sample agendas:

1. You have been assigned to write an important report. It is due in the boss's office tomorrow. However, if you could have an additional day, it would be a much better report. Prepare to discuss the matter with your boss.
2. A meeting with an important client has been pushed up from tomorrow to this afternoon. As a result, the report being written by your assistant is

47

needed today rather than tomorrow, as originally planned. How will you encourage your assistant to speed up the writing of the report without endangering its quality?

The two agendas pivot on the preparation of the report but are clearly diversified in terms of the time element. It should also be pointed out that when agendas are well-prepared, a dramatic tension is introduced naturally into the scenario. For example, tension will inevitably mount during the performance as the role players come to understand each other's position. Will the boss insist that the report be speeded up or will the employee be successful in convincing the boss that extra time is needed to do a good job on it? Perhaps a compromise will be made whereby the two decide to work together on the report. Whatever solution is reached, the action taken is not scripted into the agendas but left up to the players themselves.

The foregoing agendas exemplify one way a context may be shared, namely, the business office and an activity that is common in such an office. Contexts may also be shared with little or no forewarning. Such would be the case in the following situation:

> A, B, C, and D are among the many passengers on a flight across the Atlantic. They are strangers who have been assigned adjoining seats. Suddenly, someone announces that the plane is being hijacked.

How will each of the passengers react to this turn of events? Perhaps one of them is an undercover police agent. Another may have a weak heart and is taking the trip to undergo a delicate operation in another country. Yet another may have pressing business awaiting at the other end of the trip. The shared context of the transatlantic hijacking gives them a reason to interact. The way in which they interact will depend on how they use their personal agendas to interpret this unexpected happening. Because the unexpected serves as a catalyst to the creation of strategies by the participants, the agendas are never disclosed to the other participants.

Types of scenarios

The basic scenario is one that has two roles suitable for execution within one encounter:

Role A: You must return a defective toaster to the department store. Unfortunately, you have lost the purchase receipt and you have only your lunch hour to take care of the matter. Prepare yourself for an encounter with the salesclerk.

Role B: You are a salesclerk in the hardware department of a large store. You have been ordered to be careful in accepting returns of merchandise that may not have been purchased at the store. Prepare yourself to deal with someone who is approaching you with a toaster.

Since role A does not have much time to return the toaster, we can anticipate the use of some strategies to hasten the discussion. In addition, role A will have to be ready to say something if asked for proof of purchase. Role B may become suspicious of anyone who is in a hurry to complete such a transaction. The conversation between the two parties will naturally contain counteracting strategies. Who will prevail, if anyone, cannot be predicted, nor should it be.

As indicated previously, the agendas of the roles are not mutually known. Role A does not know about the directive given to B to be wary of customers without purchase receipts. Role B is not told that A has lost the receipt and is in a hurry. The need to disambiguate each other's agenda is the usual first step in scenarios of this type. Inevitably the participants will apply their own value judgments in interpreting motives. Is the individual with the toaster to be trusted? How will B answer to the store manager if it turns out that the toaster was not purchased at the store? Role A, in turn, may wonder why B is so reluctant to refund money or replace the toaster. Participants in a well-founded scenario soon discover that they cannot simply play out prescribed roles. They cannot take for granted that they will achieve their goals simply by acting out conventional or stock lines supplied by the text or the teacher.

If the rehearsal phase has been productive for the groups preparing the scenario, each will have scripted out several strategic pathways to follow in order to execute its particular game plan. For example, the group preparing A will have anticipated a claim by B that all appliances are checked before being sold in order to ensure that they work properly. A may also be prepared for the possibility that B will be in no great hurry to complete the transaction. B, on the other hand, may want to have something ready to counter an accusation that the store is being unfair to its customers. Even more importantly, B will need a number of questions to ask A in order to determine the legitimacy of the refund.

The variables affecting the performance of the students playing A and B are too numerous for the teacher to control or even anticipate. These variables include the students' state of preparedness, how they happen to feel that day, and certainly how they will react to each other once they begin to perform. Such matters should not concern the teacher. It is soon apparent that the same scenario will never be acted out in identical ways twice in a row. This variability is a strength of the scenario as a pedagogical device. It enables learners to fit the target language to their own preferences.

Here are other examples of the basic two-role scenario:

Scenario Title: Surprise! Surprise!

Role A: You are preparing for a final exam, which will be given tomorrow. It is evening and your friend calls you to invite you over for a while. What will you do? Should you keep studying? Do you need a break? You know that this friend loves to talk and may keep you there for hours.

Role B: It is close to the end of the college semester and today is the birthday of your friend (A). You and your other friends have organized a surprise birthday party for A. You know that A may be studying for finals, but it is your job to call him or her up and extend an invitation to come over to your place, where the party will be. Of course, you cannot reveal the real purpose for your invitation.

The idea with this scenario is to put A in the position of having to choose between work and play, while thrusting upon B the responsibility of carrying off an event involving many others. The questions posed to A are intended to help him or her become better aware of what factors might influence the decision. These questions may be omitted if the teacher feels that the role is clear enough for the player. By the same token, B need not be reminded that the real purpose of the invitation is to be kept a secret.

Scenario Title: After All, What Are Friends For?

Role A: Your friend has just bought a new car and has left it in your care while on a business trip. Knowing that you are also in the market for a new car, your friend has given you permission to drive it. On one of your excursions with the car, it stalls in a deserted place. You go for help. When you return, you find that someone has smashed in the side and has left the scene of the accident. Explain what happened to your friend.

Role B: You have just bought a new car. You must take a business trip, so you leave the car in the care of a friend. This friend is also interested in buying a new car, so you give your friend permission to try out your car during your absence. Your friend doesn't know it, but if he or she buys a car from the dealer who sold you your car, you will receive a sales commission. You have returned from your trip and now you ask your friend how he or she liked the car.

In this scenario, A may feel somewhat guilty for the damage done to the car. On the other hand, the car did stall, and if B wants A to buy a similar car, some argument must be advanced to diminish the importance of that fact when it comes up in the discussion.

Scenario Title: An Offer That Is Hard to Refuse

Role A: You are on a business trip to a new city. Your company has provided you with an expense account and has made a reservation for you in a hotel. You hail a cab at the airport and ask the driver to take you to this hotel. The driver recommends another hotel that is superior to the hotel where you have your reservation. What will you do? What will you ask the driver, if anything, about the hotel being recommended?

Role B: You drive a cab in a big city. You have an arrangement with a hotel whereby you receive a fee for every out-of-town visitor who takes a room on your recommendation. You have just picked up a passenger at the airport who asks to be taken to a rival hotel. What will you say to convince this person to go to the hotel where you receive a commission?

The traveler may or may not be inclined to take the driver's recommendation. If so inclined, then several questions would need to be asked concerning the room rates, the location of the hotel, and the quality of lodging there as compared to the other hotel. If not inclined, then the traveler has to be prepared to give some counterstrategies to the enticements of the driver. The driver must be ready with a convincing sales pitch or at least with some reasons for checking into the hotel he or she is recommending.

Multiple-role scenarios

It is possible to involve more than two roles in a scenario, provided that each is given a distinct reason for being involved. The use of a third party simply as a background for the actions of the two main participants does not promote a multiple-role interaction. The following is an example of a scenario where three different parties interact:

Scenario Title: A Parting of the Ways?

Role A: You have been offered a lucrative job in a foreign country. You must go there alone for three years, or, if you marry, your spouse may accompany you. You have a fiance(e) (role C) and also an invalid parent (role B) who depends on you for help. What will you do? Discuss the offer with your parent and your fiance(e).

Role B: You are a widow(er) who has a son/daughter (role A). This son/daughter has been helping you get around. However, you have met a widowed person of the opposite sex who wants the two of you to live together and combine your pension checks. Marriage is not in the picture. Explain this situation to your son/daughter and ask for advice.

Role C: You have just been promoted. Your new position requires you to move to another city. Will you accept the promotion? Discuss the matter with your fiance(e) (role A), who has an invalid parent as a responsibility.

In keeping with the criteria of shared context but separate agendas, the roles in this scenario are interconnected but are also endowed with distinct situations to resolve. A has the chance to make a good salary and perhaps enjoy a new living experience in another country. However, A also has the responsibility of the invalid parent and the tie to the fiance(e). B has been given an offer that is attractive although clouded by potential disapproval by A because of the unorthodoxy of the arrangement and the problem of being an invalid. C is facing the dilemma of whether to move up in the firm and perhaps break off with a fiance(e) or remain in the same position. Yet another option will become apparent to C once the interaction begins, namely, marrying A and going with him or her to the foreign country. This particular scenario could be performed either as a multiple-role one or as two dyadic ones (A–B, A–C).

Group scenarios

In group scenarios, students are allowed to react in their own ways to an event or set of circumstances that involves all of them. The purse-snatcher scenario described in Chapter 2 is an example of a group scenario. The hijacking episode cited earlier in this chapter is another. The following is similar to the purse-snatcher scenario in that it can be used at very basic levels of instruction.

Scenario Title: The Snake in the Sack

Execution: This scenario takes place on a bus. Seven to eight students are asked to arrange their seats as if they were passengers. One student can be asked to play the part of the bus driver. The teacher plays a passenger who gets on the bus carrying a sack or a large bag. The teacher sits down for a while, holding the sack on his or her lap. Then the teacher rises and places the sack on the seat just vacated. If well-timed, the sack will pop open to reveal an inflated rubber snake extending its head. As the student-passengers react to the snake, the teacher provides the target language equivalents for what they would like to say. Likely expressions include "Eek, a snake!" "Is it poisonous?" and "Throw it out the window!" (Inflatable rubber snakes can be obtained through mail-order catalogs or purchased from garden supply stores.)

The conversation that results from this scenario can be written on the blackboard and used as the basis for the debriefing that follows the performance. The rationale for using such a scenario at the beginning level of second-language study is to provide a setting in which learners can react in fairly uncomplicated utterances to a situation they all share. The teacher serves as a pivot for the conversation by introducing the key element in the situation.

Scenario Title: The Contest

Execution: Students are divided into two teams and told that they are about to compete in a contest. In this contest, the team getting the most correct answers will win a prize (usually a bag of candy purchased ahead of time by the teacher). Any matter relating to the geography or history or culture of the target-language country can be used as the basis of the contest. In one version of this scenario, a map of the country can be displayed and the teacher can write the names of each of its major states or provinces on the board. Alongside each of these states, the teacher writes the name of its capital city. While the writing goes on, the students can be taken through an oral drill in which they repeat the names after the teacher. If the students are rank beginners, the teacher can supply some key vocabulary, such as "capital city" or "province" and the equivalent for "What is the capital city of ...?." After each state and city are written on the board and the oral drill is completed, the city names are erased and the contest begins. The teacher calls out the states and marks down the points for each team that responds with the correct answer before the other team does. What the participants do not know is that the teacher has given all the correct answers to a confidante before the contest. The confidante has been instructed to give all the correct answers to one of the teams. The answers are given in a blatantly open way so that the members of the losing team can observe this "cheating." After the favored team wins, the teacher presents the prize with great fanfare, lauding them as much as possible. At this point, or even earlier, members of the other team will begin to complain. They will start to say things like "That's unfair!" or "They cheated!" The teacher then tells them how to say these things in the target language and gives the other team a chance to defend itself, also within the target language. After the exchange has gone on for a few minutes, the exercise is terminated. The teacher explains that the contest was "fixed" right from the start in order to get them to speak to each other. A second bag of candy is produced and presented to the "losing" team as an equal prize for being such good sports. The contest is, of course, only a way to motivate the teams to engage in exchanges in the target language. Whatever they say to each other becomes the basis for a debriefing session.

Both of the preceding group scenarios have been used successfully in several languages and have been executed by different groups of beginning students. Although the range of expression is not a wide one, each performance is intense and therefore highly motivated.

Open-ended scenarios

Life is not simply a series of disjointed events. Some experiences take place over several interrelated episodes and are apt to involve "long-term" roles, as discussed earlier. In such cases, people choose their verbal strategies in consideration of what is shared or believed to be shared from previous encounters. With the open-ended scenario, an attempt is made to capture the continuity of such life experiences and to allow learners the opportunity to use the target language accordingly. Although the minimum number of episodes in open-ended scenarios is two, there is no limit to the maximum number they may contain. Each new episode builds upon developments that derive from the events of the previous one. The following are some examples of open-ended scenarios:

Scenario Title: Dinner for Two?

Episode 1.

Role A: (female) An important client has come to town to discuss a merger with your firm. You are being groomed for a promotion, so your boss asks you to join him and the client for dinner. You already have a dinner engagement with your fiance. Telephone him to explain why you must cancel the date.

Role B: (male) Your fiancee phones you to cancel the dinner date for this evening. How do you react to her reason for canceling it? Will you reschedule it?

Episode 2.

Role B: (continued) After your fiancee hangs up, your sister calls you to tell you that she has just come into town on a visit and would like to have dinner with you. Will you agree to take her to dinner? She has heard of a very good restaurant and would like to go there.

Role C: (female) You are on a business trip to a city where your brother lives. You have not seen him for a long time. Call him up and see if he would like to have dinner with you in a special restaurant that has been highly recommended by a colleague of yours.

Episode 3.

Role A: You and your boss are entertaining the client at dinner. Midway through the meal, your boss is called away on an emergency. You and the client are left alone to finish dinner. You see your fiance enter the restaurant with another woman. What do you say to him?

Role B: You and your sister enter the restaurant and you find your fiancee there with another man. What do you say to her?

Of course, for episode 3 to happen, B must be willing to have dinner with his sister. If he is unwilling, then the scenario cannot continue beyond episode 2. In either case, the criterion of being open-ended is met.

Scenario Title: The Distraught Babysitter

Episode 1.

Role A: You are a teenager. You have been offered your first babysitting job. You really want the money. Your mother has to give her permission. Discuss it with her.

Role B: Your teenager has been offered a babysitting job. It will be his or her first job – providing you give your permission. Will you do so? There is an important test coming up at school tomorrow.

Episode 2.

Role A: The woman who hired you to be her babysitter tells you that she and her husband will be at a very important reception. The baby has not been feeling well but has been given some medicine and is now sleeping peacefully. A number is left for you to call if there is any serious difficulty. Otherwise, she and her husband must not be called away from the reception. Two hours after the woman and her husband leave, the baby awakens and begins to cough. The cough will not stop and the baby seems to be choking. What will you do? Who will you call?

The other role in episode 2 depends on who is called by the babysitter. It can be the babysitter's mother, in which case role B is the following:

Role B: Your teenager calls you from the home where he or she is babysitting to tell you that the baby seems to be very ill and is choking. What advice do you give? Should the hospital be called? What can you do to help?

If the mother of the baby is chosen, then the following role is appropriate:

Role B: The babysitter calls you to tell you that the baby seems to be ill and is choking. What do you do? Will you leave this important reception? Is there any advice you can give the babysitter?

Data-based scenarios

The following is an example of how information can be meted out to the participants to lead them to react to conditions in which important data change:

Scenario Title: A Diet Gone Astray

Roles A and B: (both supplied with the same information) You have been put on a diet by your physician. Each must lose 15 pounds. The physician weighs each of you every two weeks. You are asked to give a reason to both the doctor and your friend for the weight that you register for that period. Here are your weights:

A: Original weight – 150
   First two weeks – 145
B: Original weight – 152
   First two weeks – 143

Each ensuing episode brings out a different weight:

A: second two weeks – 146
B: second two weeks – 141
A: third two weeks – 146
B: third two weeks – 140

The information about the weights is shared openly; it is manipulated so that one participant is not doing so well on the diet while the other is having great success. This situation gives one the chance to play sympathizer or teaser, while the other has to be defensive. However, at this point, the weights can be turned around so that the one losing weight starts to gain it back again and the other begins to lose:

A: fourth two weeks – 141
B: fourth two weeks – 146

In addition to being data-based, this scenario is also open-ended and, in fact, can be carried through as many episodes as desired by the teacher.

Many contemporary ESL and foreign-language texts utilize facsimiles or copies of street maps, bus schedules, and newspaper ads as the bases for various exercises. For example, an ad for an apartment may be accompanied by questions that direct the student to extract important information from it. Although such exercises are probably effective as far as they go, they are not inherently strategic. However, they can be adapted so that they become the database for scenarios. For example, the apartment seeker can be offered an excellent apartment, with the restriction that no pets are allowed. The only problem given to the student playing the apartment seeker is that a friend has entrusted him or her with the care of her dog for a few weeks. Will the owner of the apartment accept the provisional stay of this pet? What arguments can the potential renter advance? For the role of the apartment owner, it could be stated that this particular person is the only one who has responded to the ad in over three weeks and the mortgage payment is overdue.

Another example of a data-based scenario is entitled "An Honest Face at Customs." This scenario can be presented in several versions. In one version, a traveler about to pass through customs observes that the customs officer has caught someone trying to enter the country with more local currency than is allowed. Our traveler realizes that he or she also has more than the limit of local currency and must now face the same customs officer. The task for the traveler is to be prepared to answer the officer's questions. The officer's role card should note that the encounter with the person who was trying to pass customs with the extra currency has resulted in a backup. Other travelers have begun to complain that they are about to miss connecting flights within the country. As a result, the customs officer must be more expeditious but not less careful in facing the remaining travelers.

In another version of the same scenario, the customs officer is told that one of the travelers has more currency than is allowed, and the task is to interrogate each one in order to find the guilty party. A further restriction is that the interrogation must be fairly quick in order to allow the honest travelers to pass through customs in time to catch connecting flights. In this version of the scenario, a cache of play money is given to the group of students playing the travelers. This group is allowed to decide which of their members will carry the money and what each will say to the officer.

Although this next scenario has three roles, two of them (B and C) can be prepared together in one rehearsal group.

Scenario Title: **Give Me the News Straight!**

Role A: (male) You've just had a serious heart attack and are confined to the hospital. Your wife and your doctor seem to know more about your condition and chances for survival than they are willing to tell you. Work out a plan to get them to tell you exactly what your chances are for a full recovery.

Role B (wife) and Role C (doctor): B's husband has had a heart attack and is confined to a hospital bed. Meanwhile, he doesn't know it, but he has just won the national lottery and is now a rich man. Work out a plan to tell him this news without exciting him so much that he will suffer another attack.

In one student performance the doctor asked the patient: "What would you do if you won a million dollars?" The patient's response was: "I would give you half of it," which caused the doctor to have a heart attack. The students decided to turn the performance into a skit by writing down the script after participating in the scenario themselves and watching others perform in it. Although such an exercise was not required, it contributed to the students' sense of control over discourse in the target language.

Strategic interaction

The following scenarios are addressed to elementary and secondary-level school children enrolled in ESL and foreign-language courses. Although the subject matter is adolescent, the interplay between the roles is just as strategic as that of the scenarios presented earlier in this chapter.

Scenario Title: The Goldfish and the Rabbit

Role A: You are looking after your friend's goldfish while he or she is on vacation with the rest of the family. Unfortunately, the fish dies suddenly. Your mother replaces it with another one that is almost identical to it. Perhaps your friend will not notice the replacement. Prepare yourself for what your friend might say when you return the goldfish.

Role B: Your friend is looking after your pet goldfish while you are on vacation. During your trip, your father buys you a rabbit. Your mother says, however, that you can have only one pet – either the goldfish or the rabbit. Perhaps your friend will take one of your pets. Which one do you prefer to have?

Scenario Title: Just a Little Longer, Mom!

Role A: You are watching a good movie on TV, but it is getting late and your mother wants you to go to bed. What will you say to her to convince her to let you continue watching TV?

Role B: Your child stays up late to watch TV whenever given the chance to do so. He or she must go to bed in order to be wide awake in school the next day. What will you say to make your child go to bed?

Scenario Title: The Circus Is in Town!

Role A: You have much homework to do but you want to go to the circus. Maybe you can convince your father to take you.

Role B: You must go to work but your child wants to go to the circus. What will you do?

Scenario Title: Don't Cry!

Role A: Your younger sister is playing with your favorite toy. If you take it away from her, she will cry and your mother will scold you. What will you say to your sister in order to get your toy back?

Role B: Your older sister doesn't like you to play with her toys. When you take one, she gets angry and takes it back. What will you say to her so that you can keep playing with a toy that you just took from her room?

It should not be a matter of concern to the teacher that in some of the adolescent scenarios, children are given an adult role to play. In our own classroom observations, it is clear that children enjoy assuming adult roles, which they can interpret in their own fashion.

The effect of social convention on role options

It is to be expected that the particular conventions of a society will impose certain constraints on the options for action open to a role player. In fact, roles are sometimes composed so that they lead the player to concentrate on conforming to the expectations of politeness. Consider the following:

> You are seated on a bus. An elderly lady enters, loaded down with packages. There are no free seats. What will you do?

The intention is to get the role player to follow the social protocol of being polite to elderly people who seem in need of help in public places. No real options for other actions are open. It is possible, however, to address social constraints while still providing for diverse options. Let us change the role to the following:

> You are not feeling well. You catch a bus to get to the doctor's office. You are relieved to find that there is one free seat on the bus and you take it. An elderly woman gets on the bus at the next stop, loaded down with packages. She stands in front of you. What will you do? Will you give her your seat? What will you say to her?

The pressure of social convention remains a factor in this revised version of the role, but the introduction of a personal concern (the role player's supposedly delicate state of health) opens up other options: (1) explaining to the elderly person that illness prevents relinquishing the seat or (2) making an offer to hold the elderly person's packages for her, so that both parties will share the inconvenience brought on by the lack of unoccupied seats on the bus.

Other kinds of role play

Scripted roles

In some exercises with pairs of roles, the outline of a script is given to each player. Abbs (1980: 219) provides an illustration of what can be done with scripted roles:

(1) *General Instruction*: It is Sunday afternoon. You have nothing to do and are bored. Telephone a friend. Work in pairs.
(2) *Script to follow*: YOUR PARTNER: Answer the phone
    YOU: Say who you are.   and say your
                                            name.

Strategic interaction

YOU: Ask if your friend is busy... YOUR PARTNER: Say you are busy...

Such an activity highlights the various mechanisms (use of openers and closers and the taking of turns) that are needed to manage conversation. In scenarios, such mechanisms are addressed during rehearsals and debriefings, as they relate to actual performances.

Simulations

Simulations constitute another class of pedagogical devices related to scenarios. In the definition given to them by Jones (1982: 5), they are called "realities of function in a simulated and structured environment." Like strategic interaction scenarios, simulations draw from credible real-life happenings. Another way in which simulations are like scenarios is the care taken not to let each player know what position the others are taking in the interaction. In a manner of speaking, simulations are like elaborated or open-ended scenarios because they bring about an inter-relating of roles over several episodes.

Among the illustrations given by Jones (1982) of simulations is one about the difficulty caused in a school district by the introduction of a new teaching method. Involved in the simulation are teachers and school inspectors called to evaluate the new method. Each is given a role card specifying the obligations of that particular social role, the understanding of the case, and a position to take (e.g., "I have nothing against the simulation technique as such... "). Jones makes the point that simulations are not games, because the intent is not to win but to use the various functions of language. Jones (1983) has provided a number of simulations for intermediate and advanced students of English as a foreign language. Crookall (1985) discusses both the theory and practice of simulations.

There are some differences between simulations and scenarios. Simulations usually require a greater number of students to perform. In fact, every member of the class may be asked to prepare and perform a different role. Although the whole class may participate in a scenario, its efforts are usually directed to the preparation of a small number of roles. A more important difference between simulations and scenarios is that a simulation role card is apt to specify a particular position that the performer is expected to articulate. Scenario roles, on the other hand, will specify situational details but will leave the course of action open to the performer.

The teacher in a simulation plays the important role of "controller," with the main obligation to keep the action moving. In the strategic interaction approach, the teacher changes roles several times, from counselor (during the rehearsal phase) to orchestrator (for the performance phase) to discussion leader (in the debriefing phase).

Sociodrama is yet another pedagogical device related to the scenario. In sociodrama, a story is told in order to build dramatic tension. Scarcella (1983) gives an example in which a newlywed invites her mother-in-law to celebrate the latter's birthday by sharing some dessert. While the mother-in-law (who, we are told in the story, disapproved of the marriage of this woman to her son) is seated in the living room, the newlywed discovers that her cake has burned in the oven. Some sort of explanation or excuse must be made or some diversionary tactic must be found by the newlywed. The story stops with the daughter-in-law offering her mother-in-law another drink while the latter comments that she doesn't want another drink and is ready to eat some cake. At this point, students are allowed to consider what solutions they would offer. The teacher then selects students who have given solutions, and they are asked to act out these solutions in front of the class. As in strategic interaction, the enactments are then discussed and alternative ways of solving the problem are explored. Reenactments with new solutions may follow the discussion period.

Roles in the case method

Jacobson (1984) describes an approach to teaching content courses known as the "case method" (see also Christenson 1981). This approach is currently enjoying popularity in American business schools and law schools. The major themes and issues of the field in question are presented as problems to be discussed by the students. The teacher leads the discussion, fielding questions and rephrasing commentary wherever necessary. In some ways, the case is like a scenario. Both lead to multiple solutions from the same set of givens. Both promote the sense of immediacy and plausibility of the surrounding circumstances. Perhaps one difference between scenarios and cases can be found in the use of the latter to favor one or more solutions over others. Scenarios are not intended to be judgmental in this way because our major interest lies in enhancing the use of the target language and not in promoting one solution over another.

Roles in sociodrama

Sociodrama resembles strategic interaction in its division of pedagogical and performance activities (i.e., both sociodrama and strategic interaction provide the opportunity for students to discuss the "dilemma," perform it, and then discuss the performance). A scenario can be derived rather easily from the sample sociodrama provided by Scarcella:

Role A: Your son has married a woman in another country and you have not had the chance to meet her until now. She invites you for a meal so that you can get to know each other. How will you react? What will you say to her?

Role B: You have invited your mother-in-law to dinner (you are a newlywed and this is her first visit to your house). While she is sitting in the living room, you discover that your roast has burned. What will you say to your mother-in-law?

In our derived scenario, the mother-in-law is not told of her daughter-in-law's problem. More importantly, she is given the freedom to form her own attitude toward her daughter-in-law.

How to write scenarios

The key to writing scenarios is to let your imagination run free. Have you ever sat in a restaurant or on a park bench or in the lounge of a busy airport and casually watched the people around you? Fellow diners, strollers, travelers – all on a par with you but without names or any history known to you. Try this game.

Step 1: Conjecture as to what each does for a living. Here comes a man in his middle thirties. He is walking slowly and is carrying a briefcase and small overnight bag that will fit under the seat of the airplane. He is dressed in a business suit that is somewhat wrinkled. He has the look of being accustomed to taking short trips, an observation supported by the small overnight bag. Quite possibly he is a salesman who has been working at his current job for some time. Is he going to or returning from a business meeting? My guess is that his wrinkled suit indicates that he is on his way home.

Another young man comes along. He, too, is wearing a business suit. However, his suit bears the signs of having just come off a clothes hanger. Although slightly out of fashion, the suit looks hardly worn. Perhaps he doesn't wear it often. You look at his hands. They are rough and calloused. No salesman, certainly. He is probably a manual laborer and is on a trip he rarely takes. Is he off on a vacation? No, his attire is too formal for that. Perhaps he is being transferred to another location by his firm, an international company that has plants in several countries.

You now notice a young woman. She is carrying a large bag and rolled-up charts or posters under her arm. She is dressed very fashionably. A designer? Perhaps. An elderly woman crosses your line of vision, wearing a corsage and carrying a book. The title is in bold print: *The Art of Renaissance Florence*. A tourist, most likely on her way to visit Italy. Her family or her friends have just given her a send-off – that would explain the corsage.

After you have played this game for a while you realize that you may be far off the track in your assessments and you can't look at the back of a book for the correct answers. Nevertheless, the game helped you pass the time and, more importantly, it has fired up your imagination.

It is time for *step* 2: Pick several of the people you have observed and build a story around them. The man with the hanger-creased suit and the rough hands might have a special skill. He is the only one who knows how to fix a highly complicated piece of machinery that operates cranes. He has been called upon to use his expertise at a bridge-construction site in the Andean mountains of South America, where a crane has broken down in the process of transporting an injured worker from a precipitous cliff. Despite the need for caution, he will want to complete this assignment as soon as possible in order to return to the bedside of his ailing wife who must undergo delicate heart surgery very soon.

The elderly woman wearing the corsage and carrying the travel book is really an operative for the CIA. Her innocuous appearance helps to disguise the real purpose of her visit to Europe: to give special instructions to an undercover agent who is trying to unearth a "mole" in the spy network. She has ostensibly retired from an office job at CIA headquarters in Langley, Virginia. Not even her family is aware of the real purpose of her trip. Her assignment is fraught with dangers. The last contact person disappeared last year on a flight to Europe and has not been heard from since.

If step 1 was pure conjecture, step 2 is full fantasy. The effects on you, however, are considerable. Suddenly there is excitement all around you. The people that pass by are no longer nonentities. Most important of all, you now realize that you can put your observational powers to use in activating your imagination. Now the third and final step.

Step 3: Imagine an event that could involve you and those around you. For example, an announcement comes over the loudspeaker advising all passengers that the flight you are about to take has been overbooked. Some of you will have to remain behind. What would you do if you were (a) the CIA agent, (b) the troubleshooting expert, or any other imagined character? What arguments would you present to the airline representative? Indeed, how about your own reasons for traveling, whatever they might be? Could you postpone your trip? If you were the airline representative, what counterarguments would you make?

Any number of potential dialogs could arise in your thoughts. That is a good sign. You are on your way to preparing yourself for writing scenario themes. You don't really have to be in an airport or a restaurant or anywhere other than your own room in order to embark on such flights of imagination. The next task is to pare down restrictions on each personage so that your students can assume the roles without being forced to take on attitudes and positions in which they might not believe.

Scenarios from real life

The events of real life can sometimes be very accommodating to the language teacher. How often have you found yourself enmeshed in a situation that was very serious at the time but in retrospect is humorous? You had to make a choice on what course of action to follow. Perhaps the choice was difficult when you made it but now is no longer a threatening one. Suppose, for instance, your husband has arranged to have your portrait painted by a well-known artist. You arrive at his studio ready for your first sitting and you discover that he paints only nudes. Since your husband went to considerable bother to contract with this artist, will you let yourself be painted in the nude? Will you argue with the artist in an effort to convince him to paint you in your clothes? Does this scene strike you as being farfetched? It actually took place, as recounted to me by one of the teachers attending a strategic interaction training session. Think this situation over and you will be able to see several roles in a derivative scenario. Perhaps the interaction should take place between the husband (who has made the arrangement with the artist but does not know that he paints only nudes) and the wife (who has discovered this fact and must discuss the matter with her husband before agreeing to it). Perhaps some confrontation with the artist can be worked out.

Newspaper articles in the human interest section of the paper can also be a rich source of material for scenario themes. The founder of a department store catering to the rich recounted in an interview with a reporter the instance when the manager of his fur department became involved in a wager with a customer. It seems that this customer, a well-to-do woman, was in the market for a new fur coat. The one that she liked was overpriced, she thought. After the fur department manager insisted that the price was proper, she made a friendly wager with him to the effect that if he could sell the coat at his stated price within a week's time, she would buy another at the same price. If he could not, she would be sold this coat at a much lower price. A few days later, the fur department manager learned from his salesclerk that the coat had been sold and at the announced price. His joy at winning the wager was diminished, however, when he also learned that the purchaser of the coat was none other than his customer's husband. To make matters worse, the coat was delivered to the home of another woman!

This story can be highly productive as a scenario. One way in which it is especially effective is as a group scenario for advanced students. The teacher begins by selecting one person to play the fur manager and another to play the customer. The background is explained to the two of them in front of the class – up to the point where the wager is made over the price of the coat. Then, the student playing the customer is asked to leave the room. While she is absent, the teacher explains what has happened after the wager was made: The coat was sold to the customer's husband, but was delivered to another woman. The class is asked to help the "manager" decide what to do and what to say to the "customer." Together, they explore several possibilities and their likely results. When they get to a juncture where they think they have worked out a solution, or when they realize that they cannot work out a solution, the teacher calls the "customer" back into the room, to confront the "manager." Of course, the "customer" wishes to know the outcome of the wager. Did she win? Will she get the fur coat at a discounted price? The tension builds as the class observes what the "manager" will say.

In a different treatment of the same theme, the information for each part played by the principal figures in the scenario is written on role cards and distributed to different players. (I am indebted to James Lantolf for the variation of the scenario.) As in the usual practice of preparing scenario roles, the student playing the customer is told that she has made a wager with the manager. Another student, playing the husband's role, is told that he has bought a coat for a woman friend (motive unstated). Yet another student can play the part of the friend who receives the coat. Only the sales manager is told all the information. He is the one who can orchestrate interactions by bringing different people together as he and the class see fit.

This particular scenario has been used often and in many different foreign-language classes. It has inspired students to produce much discourse in the target language and to attempt diverse solutions. The scenario can be given as homework in the following format, illustrated in French:

Le manteau de fourrure: Vous êtes directeur de département-fourrure d'un magasin de mode très connu. Une femme riche qui est une cliente ordinaire essaie un très beau manteau de fourrure. Vous lui dites qu'il lui va bien. Elle répond qu'elle l'achèterait mais que le prix de $20,000 est trop élevé. Vous lui répondez que le prix est juste et que vous le vendrez à ce prix sans difficulté. Elle fait alors un pari avec vous que si vous le vendez avant une semaine, elle vous en achètera un autre au même prix. Vous acceptez le pari. La seule preuve de vente qu'elle exige est le nom de l'acheteur. Au bout de quelques jours le vendeur vous informe que le manteau a été vendu. Quand vous demandez le nom de l'acheteur, vous découvrez que c'est le mari de la femme avec qui vous avez fait le pari. Cependant, l'addresse où le manteau a été livré est celle d'une autre femme.

Questions

1. Que faites-vous? ('What will you do?')
2. Direz-vous à la femme ce qui est arrivé? ('Will you tell the woman what happened?')

3. **Parlerez-vous au mari? à l'autre femme?** ('Will you speak to the husband? to the other woman?')
4. **Annulerez-vous le pari?** ('Will you call off the bet?')
Ecrivez un dialogue entre vous et n'importe lequel des trois protagonistes de l'histoire. ('Write a dialogue between yourself and any of the other persons in the story.')

In this particular assignment, the student is given a choice not only of what solution to seek but also with whom to interact. The teacher's traditional concerns are with vocabulary and structure in such an exercise. The key words are included: *le manteau de fourrure* ('fur coat'), *le pari* ('wager'), *cliente ordinaire* ('regular customer'), and so on, but they are not given as a detached list. They come as the expected components of a text. The questions given at the end of the text are intended to jog the student's imaginative processes rather than demand a direct answer. The real exercise lies in leading the student to execute strategies and do a credible job of role portrayal.

Summary

The scenario is the key device in making second-language discourse strategic in the classroom. It contains four essential elements: strategic interplay, roles, personal agendas, and shared context. In presenting the scenario we highlight spontaneity in discourse. The roles played by students in scenarios are multifaceted. Some roles are determined by social convention and include "vendors," "shoppers," and "travelers." Others are psychological in disposition (such as "friend," "rival," and "competitor"). Roles may be either overt (i.e., marked by location, activity, and/or manner of dress) or covert (determined largely by interaction). Some roles function in complementary sets (e.g., vendor/customer). Others are noncomplementary (e.g., salesperson/window-shopper). Role complementation or the lack of it has an effect on the type of verbal exchange generated. Conversations between complementary roles are likely to be more conventionalized than those between noncomplementary roles. In order to make the discourse purposeful, each role is given an agenda to fulfill. Finally, role players should be placed in a shared context so that their agendas will not suffer from mutual incoherence.

The basic scenario consists of two roles that interact. Multiple-role scenarios are also used to good advantage. Group scenarios are those in which the participants are led to react to a common experience without a rehearsal period. Open-ended scenarios allow for diverse episodes to be enacted as the role players are placed in new circumstances that develop from previous encounters. Data-based scenarios are built around factual information or props to which each party reacts. Scenarios can be used with students at any level. When used with children, the subject matter is adjusted to reflect concerns that are suitable to their age level. Scenarios share some features with other types of instructional devices (such as role plays and simulations). The differences between scenario roles and standard role plays can be summed up as follows:

Role Play	*Scenario Role*
1. Student is given a "part"; student portrays someone other than self.	1. Student plays self within the framework of the role.
2. Student is often told what to do or think (e.g., you want to go to the movies but your partner doesn't).	2. Student is given a situation but not told what to think or do.
3. The target language is used to practice previously presented items, thereby reinforcing the syllabus.	3. Aspects of the target language are taken from the interaction and determine the linguistic syllabus.
4. Usually all the players know what the others will say and do.	4. The interaction contains a greater element of uncertainty and dramatic tension.

The writing of scenarios requires the utilization of one's imagination about life in general. A good outside source of scenario themes can be found in real-life happenings.

4 Rehearsing and performing the scenario

It can be said that the use of strategic interaction in the classroom serves to "defuse" the potentially stressful occurrences that often happen to foreign-language learners when they become involved in real-life circumstances. This chapter covers the first two steps in this defusing process: rehearsing and performing scenarios.

Much lip service has been paid to "learner-centered" instruction in the current literature on methodology. Although such an orientation is highly valued today, few teachers seem prepared to deal with the effects of "loosening the reins" on their students. We must surely wonder how a course of instruction can be learner-centered if the teacher still dominates all interactions. The classroom in which students direct their own learning can be noisy. It may even appear to be disorganized to the outside observer. But we must put appearances aside and let our students work through the normal course of events leading to scenario execution. Rehearsal is the first major point of reference in the overall organization of our interactive classroom (see Chapter 8 for an illustration of all three phases of strategic interaction).

Rehearsal

The rehearsal begins when different roles in a scenario are assigned to groups of students, *one role per group*. If possible, allow students to form their own groups, rather than impose an arrangement on them (a justification for self-assignment is given below). One caveat: Try to keep the size of each group to no more than eight students. Larger groups hinder communication among members and may break into smaller divisions. Depending on the size of the class, the instructor should have sufficient scenarios so that separate roles can be assigned to each small group. For example, in a class of 42 (a large one by current measures, to be sure), three two-role scenarios would suffice to allow each of six groups of seven students to have its own role. The breakdown would be as follows:

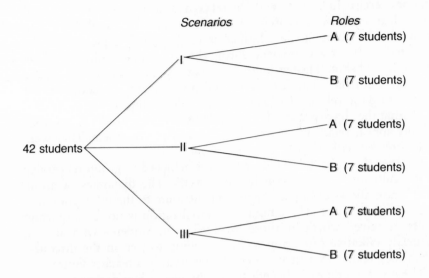

Role assignments in large classes

Role groups should form circles so that they can build solidarity throughout the rehearsal period. The circle arrangement also helps them to shield themselves from discussions going on in the surrounding groups. It is a good idea to locate the groups so that the A's and B's of each scenario are spatially distant from each other. Role group IA, for example, could be separated from role group IB by placing role group IIIA between them, and so on. An easy way to make this arrangement is to have the groups form first and then distribute the roles so that adjoining groups have unrelated roles. In classes with fewer students, the teacher may have to locate the groups at different corners of the room. By no means should groups interact with each other during the rehearsal phase.

The benefits of group work in rehearsal

A considerable amount of linguistic and psychological theory stands in the background as support for group rehearsing. Only the most obvious and least technical points will be touched on here. First of all, discussing a shared concern with peers in a nonthreatening setting reduces the anxiety sometimes felt by learners working on their own. Learners are given the freedom to ask any kind of questions they wish and make any observations they consider to be relevant. In a group of peers, no one can sound the voice of authority or demand adherence to some formal drill or exercise. In keeping with the relaxed atmosphere of the rehearsal phase, learners are free to use their own language to accomplish the task at hand. The point of the rehearsal is to develop a game plan to be executed in the target language during the coming performance phase. The rehearsal should last as long as student interest in preparing a game plan does not flag. The teacher should not feel any reluctance about terminating the rehearsal whenever the students appear to be satisfied with what they have prepared. In actual observation, groups in rehearsal usually appear relaxed. Laughter often emanates from them. They seem to be imbued with a spirit of cooperation.

Another theoretical desideratum that is achieved in group rehearsing is the cultivation of different learning styles. The dynamics of group interaction allows each participant to contribute to the interaction in a wide range of ways. The amount of verbalization is not as important as its perceived worth by those involved in it. Students who are not naturally talkative often appear more willing to join in the discourse when they realize that they are not dominated by a teacher figure.

There is a therapeutic benefit to be obtained when people work together on a shared topic, as borne out in the field of counseling. In the 1950s, Charles Curran found curative powers in group interaction through use of diverse languages. He also discovered a special bonus when his patients learned the foreign languages assigned to them as communicative "shields" (see Curran 1976). Stevick (1980) points out that one of the major factors hindering the learning of a new language is fear or apprehension about performing in it. Letting students discuss the performance before it takes place allays this fear to a considerable extent.

Bruffee (1984) provides a rationale in philosophical terms for the benefits of collaborative learning in groups. Charged with the same task and equipped with more or less the same skills, the members of a rehearsal group engage in a kind of discourse that can be highly efficient. This efficiency stems from the shared set of conventions as to what is relevant to the task and what constitutes progress toward completing it. By pooling their resources, the members of the group become what Bruffee calls "a community of knowledgeable peers." As peers, they become powerful agents for generating new knowledge, which they then share among themselves. Through the skill and partnership of conversation, each member of the group learns how to play him- or herself silently. In this way, the knowledge that they have gained in the company of others is internalized (see also Donato 1985).

Yet another support for group work in learning comes from the field of social psychology and is found specifically in Giles's "accommodation theory" (Giles and Smith 1979). According to Giles, four principles guide social interaction: similarity-attraction, social exchange, casual attribution, and intergroup distinctiveness. Similarity-attraction and intergroup distinctiveness relate to groups in rehearsal, while social exchange and casual attribution have a bearing on performance. Similarity-attraction states that people are attracted to those with whom they feel familiarity. Allowing students to seek out their own groups with whom to work improves the chances that they will be productive in their learning tasks. Once the group is formed, the individual's need for a social identity leads to a search for the distinctiveness of that group over others (intergroup distinctiveness). In the context of the foreign-language classroom, the importance of fluent and accurate target-language use in establishing this distinctiveness is highlighted. When the performance phase begins, the other two principles become operable: social exchange, by which each person seeks to obtain a personal benefit from the interaction, and casual attribution, by which each becomes aware of the role he or she is playing and makes an effort to deploy verbal and nonverbal language appropriate to that role.

There is yet another potential value to group work. By having students collaborate with each other, the teacher gives the proper respect to the students' own linguistic resources. Each student contributes his or her part to the collective knowledge of the group while taking from this shared wealth what can serve him or her best under the circumstances. In other words, the group shares power – if not in a fully democratic way, at least more evenly than when students must face a power-wielding teacher individually. In making this observation, we should point out a vital contrast between "power" and "control." The teacher's worth is established through the teacher's availability as a director, a source of knowledge, a helper, and a coach. To the extent that students recognize this worth, the teacher has power. Control has to do with classroom management. Even the teacher with little power in the learning process can exercise a good deal of control over the activities of the class. The good interactive teacher is well-advised to establish a personal worth by fulfilling the types of roles indicated above rather than be overly concerned with maintaining control.

Tasks for the group in rehearsal

Teachers and students working through an interactive methodology for the first time may need some direction in what they are supposed to do during the rehearsal phase. Above all, they should not assume that rehearsals are simply times when scripts are learned and predetermined parts are practiced. On the contrary, rehearsals provide the opportunity to learn much that is new. The group must complete five tasks if the rehearsal phase is to be considered a success. The teacher is faced with four complementary tasks during the same phase.

GROUP TASKS

(1) *Make certain that all group members clearly understand the charge given to them.* The charge may be written on a strip of paper and handed to the group by the teacher. In essence, the charge is a role to be formed, along with enough background information to make the setting clear. One student may read it aloud to the others, or it may be passed around to be read silently by each member of the group in turn. Having it read aloud by one member of the group may be preferable, since it enhances group solidarity.

(2) *Understand the "ground rules."* The discussion held by the group may be in either the target language or the group's native language. It may even fluctuate between the two. However, the utterances prepared for delivery during the performance must be in the target language. Members of the group may enlist each other's aid or ask the teacher at any time during rehearsal about any matter relevant to the charge. Notes may be taken and dictionaries or grammar books consulted.

(3) *Consider all options open to realizing the goal and all possible reactions to these options by the other role.* Since the conversation that will take place in the performance phase is not predictable, the group should weigh carefully the strategic value of what might be said. Counterstrategies should be readied to offset strategies that might come from the other side. If, for example, the group is charged with having to take back a defective toaster recently purchased at a department store, the store representative may claim that all sales are final. In such an eventuality, one might insist that no store has the right to sell defective merchandise. One might even include a threat to report the matter to the Better Business Bureau or some similar governmental organization that controls licenses given to stores.

(4) *Participate in choosing one member of the group to perform the role during the performance phase.* The person or persons who seem to lead the discussion during the rehearsal phase are not necessarily the same ones who should represent the group in performance. Some members of the group will appear to be better suited for performing before the class. Eventually, all members of the group are extended the opportunity to perform, but a start must be made by selecting one person. Someone may volunteer or some member may nominate another. If no representative is chosen, then the teacher will have to select a player for the performance.

(5) *Follow the steps that lead to a group decision of how to play the assigned role.* The first step is to make certain that everyone in the group understands the role and what is to be accomplished. One member of the group may read the details aloud from a slip of paper. Alternatively, slips of paper with the necessary information may be given to each group

member. The second step is a contemplative one. Each group member is required to think about the problem and weigh diverse ways to resolve it. In the third step, the group discusses various ideas proposed by individual members and anticipates the counteractions that may be taken by the other role. The group may, in fact, fluctuate between periods of discussion and contemplation until a sufficient number of ploys and counterplays have been considered. The fourth step is to decide on a "plan of action" and to pick someone to execute it during the performance stage.

TEACHER TASKS

(1) *Observe the dynamics of the groups as they form and be prepared to form the groups if the students are unable to do so.* The teacher should pay close attention to nonverbals, gaze, and body language as students form their rehearsal groups. Such communal behaviors are important indicators of the welding of a social bond among members of the group. Without this bond, group learning is not likely to be successful. Observe how members of the group arrange themselves. Are there any students who sit at some distance from the main group? Do they look away from the others during conversation? Some may position themselves at a distance but nonetheless direct their gaze toward the main group. They may wish to participate but, for some reason, are reluctant to place themselves at the center of group activity. Cultural conventions may lead some students to cast their eyes downward. Others may cross their arms over their chests. In Western countries, such a posture often signifies a reluctance to accept what is being said. People from other cultures may give different meanings to the same posture. As a result, the teacher is well advised to come to some understanding of what signals are being given by a particular set of students. Laughter is also conditioned culturally. Short bursts may indicate anxiety or initial uneasiness about participating in the group work.

(2) *Suggest options if the group appears to be stymied.* The group may not fully understand the charge or may be unable to build a game plan around it. In this case, the teacher should provide some direction by making suggestions of possible things to say. As part of the teacher's own preparation, some anticipation should be made of the various interactive routes that the scenarios might take before assigning them to the students. In this way, the teacher will be prepared to offer help when and if it is needed by the students.

(3) *Be prepared to model utterances in the target language as needed.* Students may know what they would like to say but are unable to say it in the target language. The teacher should anticipate questions of how to say things in the target language that will advance the learners' choice

of strategies. As a consequence, the teacher – especially the one who is not a native speaker of the target language – needs to prepare some utterances with diverse strategic values that can be given to the students if they ask. Of course, as the scenario is played over in different classes, the teacher will become familiar with the range of interaction needed by the students.

(4) *Give explanations as requested but do not make them lengthy.* The rehearsal phase is oriented toward the goal of realizing a game plan in the target language. Occasionally, students will ask for explanations of the grammar underlying a particular utterance. They may also want to know more about the cultural matrix of the utterance. Although it is tempting to provide full explanations for such matters, the teacher must not distract the students from their main task of preparing for the performance. If a question seems to need extensive explanation, the teacher may make a note of it and bring it up in the debriefing phase.

Something the teacher should *not* do is give the students lists of vocabulary to use in preparing the role. Lists of words and phrases, even if they are thematically appropriate, focus the students' attention on the form and structure of language rather than on the functions they are attempting to realize. Lists of words can actually be counterproductive since students sometimes feel that they *must* use the words on the lists. It is preferable to allow students to use dictionaries and textbooks to look up the words they need.

Tuning in on students' patterns of thought

As the groups rehearse their roles, it will become evident that the ways of successfully handling a controversy are many. There is no single style to be preferred over any other, and the teacher should be ready to accept whatever mode of thought seems to dominate in a given group. For example, the following scenario role may be treated in a number of different ways:

> You are a young executive in a large firm. You have invited a client to dinner in an expensive restaurant. If you can impress this client, you might win a large account and also be given a raise and a promotion by your boss. As the dinner progresses, you discover that you have left your wallet with all your money and credit cards at home. What do you do?

Some different modes of thinking about the problem are as follows:

1. *Analytic:* Outline what all the options are and decide which will be the least stressful.
2. *Idealistic:* Attempt to gain the guest's sympathy. Perhaps he or she has been in a similar situation and will understand.

3. *Pragmatic:* Be resolved to accept the situation as it is. These things do happen and perhaps one can joke about the set of circumstances.
4. *Realistic:* The problem is not really so bad, after all. Perhaps the client will lend the money. Then he or she can be asked to stop off at home for a nightcap. A check could be written and given to the client at that time.
5. *Synthesist:* The manager of this restaurant probably has had customers in similar situations before. If he can be assured of one's good intentions, the money could be sent first thing in the morning.

Of course, there is no guarantee that any of these approaches will work. The manager of the restaurant may have already formulated a policy for such situations that is potentially embarrassing to the nonpaying customer. If the dilemma is revealed to the guest, the young executive may be regarded as too inefficient and unreliable to handle major accounts. The more carefully the group reflects on all options open to them, the more focused they will make their discourse in the target language.

Cultural differences influence the style of interaction in ways that we are just beginning to understand. McCreary (1984) has traced some of the causes of breakdowns in business negotiations between Americans and Japanese to a differing view of the options available to the negotiators. English-speaking American business representatives usually take pains to distinguish among the various possible choices. Japanese business representatives, on the other hand, tend to see options as different variations of the same general solution. It is of great importance to Japanese negotiators to maintain *tatemae* ('public face'). As a result, bargaining must be done in a way that does not threaten one's dignity. Teaching Japanese to English-speaking Americans should entail a caveat against offering up sharply diverse options in negotiations, or at least give a warning that black-and-white choices may be interpreted as blunt or even insulting.

Differences in culture may be found even in the way people act in large groups. In the United States, late arrivals at a professional meeting usually attempt to enter unobtrusively and take an inconspicuous place. In Japan, a person who is late might bow and, in front of everyone, say: *domoosoku haremashita* ('It got late,' i.e., 'I'm sorry to be late') before taking a seat. Japanese extend their personal sense of formality to presenting ideas at public meetings, beginning their interventions with *tadaima* (literally, 'right now,' i.e., 'I'm going to speak now') and ending with *owari* ('the end,' or 'I'm finished').

Iranians have a social principle known as *tarof.* The goal of this principle is to be as gracious as possible. Implementing it in conversations leads speakers of the language to utter phrases that verge on the poetic.

To excuse oneself for turning away from someone at a party, one might say: "A flower has no back." *Tarof* is so pervasive that it affects the structure of entire conversations. It is not unusual for a taxi driver to refuse payment from his passengers. The driver may continue to refuse even after several offers. The passenger may have to push the money into the driver's hand and invite him, at the same time, to have a cup of tea. At this point the driver usually accepts the money and expresses regret at not having the time to drink the tea. Of course, it is understood from the beginning that the passenger should pay and that the refusal to accept the money was an instance of *tarof* in action.

It may be that every culture provides for "small talk" or "idle chatter," that is, the use of conversation to pass away the time. What is discussed on such occasions appears to vary from culture to culture. In English, for example, small talk with a stranger usually focuses on a weather theme, such as:

A: Nice weather we're having.
B: Yes, but who knows how long it'll last?

Such a theme would be alien to Italians, who prefer to discuss politics on such an occasion. For Japanese, the topic would be flowers or birds.

Thus culture can affect the not-so-obvious matters of interactive style, choice of verbal strategies, and even the topic for certain kinds of conversations. Until researchers turned their attention to the analysis of discourse, cultural awareness was an interesting but peripheral concern for teachers. It can no longer be so if we are to guide our students to generating authentic discourse in the target language.

Performance

Perhaps the most important point to make about performances in the strategic interaction approach is that they are not intended to be scenes for the entertainment of audiences. The performing students are the representatives of peer groups who share a stake with them in the outcome of the interaction. The dialog is not a staged one. It is the result of two (or more) game plans that are being executed through the medium of the target language. The outcome depends on how well the performers are able to adapt their game plans as they discover new information about each other and encounter each other's verbal strategies. The non-performing members of the groups who prepared the roles are as much involved in a dialog as those who are verbalizing it. As for the remaining students in the class – those who were not members of these groups – it is best to think of them as onlookers rather than spectators at a show. Their function is akin to that of persons witnessing an episode in real life. They are participating in a learning experience of significance because they are being called upon to make sense out of what is happening on the basis of what they are overhearing.

In essence, members of the class are cast into one of three distinct but interrelated roles during performances. They may be (1) the *scenario performers*, who go through the scenario in the target language, (2) the *group members*, who are ready to provide consultation and advice as needed by their performing representatives, or (3) the *onlookers*, who witness the performance. The teacher's participation during this phase is the multifaceted one of an *orchestrator* who sets the general framework for the interaction and calls upon the group members to give assistance to their representative in the performance whenever needed.

Setting the performance frame

Scollon and Scollon (1981: 76) use the term "performance frame" to describe the general remarks made by a narrator before launching into the details of a story. This concept is applicable to scenario performances as well, since the teacher, or one of the principals in the scenario, may say a few words about the theme of the ensuing interaction. These introductory remarks should be said in the target language, and care should be taken not to reveal the game plans of the participants. For example, the frame for a scenario involving an infirm, widowed mother and her daughter may be set as follows:

> The action takes place between a mother and her daughter over a possible change in living arrangements.

No further details should be spelled out in setting the frame. As the interaction goes on, those observing it will be exposed to such details as the invitation extended to the mother by an elderly man who wishes to live with her in order to pool their meager pensions and the offer made to the daughter of a lucrative job in a distant country. Understanding these details and the strategies worked out by the performers is an integral part of the learning experience offered in the performance stage of the scenario.

Performance prototypes

As indicated in Chapter 3, scenarios are of various types. In some, information about the roles and the intended goals of the performers is shared by those involved, but the individual game plans and the final outcome are not. In others, the intended goals and bits of background information are not made known. In scenarios like those involving dissatisfied customers and the complaint personnel of a department store,

the roles as well as the most likely goals of the performers are constrained by the setting. As a result, the performers are able to move
rather quickly to execute their game plans, without maneuvering to
discern the other's role. A complaint episode is typically like the
following:

A: May I help you?
B: Yes. This shirt I bought yesterday has a crooked seam.
A: Let me see... it looks straight to *me*.
B: No, it isn't. Look at this area here.
A: Yes, you're right. Didn't you notice it when you bought it?
B: No, it was wrapped up tightly.

At this point, A has a number of options: (1) accept the defective merchandise and authorize a refund, (2) acknowledge the defect but state
a store policy that all sales are final, or (3) offer a replacement. B will
have to decide how to react to whatever option A picks: (1) accept the
refund, (2) find a way to counter the policy of no refunds, such as
demanding to speak to the manager, or (3) insist on a refund instead of
another shirt. As soon as all options are played out, the exchange is
terminated. Whether the roles become complementary depends on the
strategy of the store's complaint officer. If this officer decides that the
customer's wish is to be met, then the conversation plays out to a more
or less formalized exchange of information.

In scenarios where the preferred outcome as well as the game plans
of the performers are not mutually understood at the outset, the performance begins with a phase of "disambiguation." The performers
engage in verbal maneuvers in order to learn as much as possible about
the general disposition of the other party before making a direct assault.
Consider the following scenario brought about by an unexpected turn
of events:

Scenario Title: Fathers Should Spend More Time with Their Sons

Role A: (mother) You had promised your 10-year-old son that you and your
husband would take him to the beach tomorrow. It is the last day of
vacation for the child. However, an old and dear friend from your
college days has called to tell you that she will be visiting
tomorrow, just for the day. The two of you have not seen each other
for twelve years. Talk with your husband and ask him if he will take
your son to the beach by himself.

Role B: (father) You and your wife have agreed to take your 10-year-old son
to the beach tomorrow. It is the last day of vacation for him and he
has wanted to go to the beach for a long time. However, your boss
has just now asked you to go golfing with him and an important
client tomorrow. Prepare to discuss this problem with your wife.
Perhaps she will take the child to the beach by herself.

The conversation between A and B may begin with a few overtures by each, playing down the significance of his or her presence at the beach. "After all," A might say, "fathers should spend more time alone with their sons." B might begin with a remark to the effect that the boss has recognized his importance in the company and has asked him to help win a big contract. B might make this statement in a happy tone, in order to enthuse A with a positive attitude about what he must eventually announce. Sooner or later, of course, each will realize that the other is preparing the ground for a change in the beach plans. When it becomes clear that each would like to be excused from the outing, the reasons for the excuses are weighed against each other. Perhaps even a compromise is possible. Depending on the time of the golfing date and the arrival of mother's friend, the family may be able to take their son to the beach for a short time. Another possibility might be for mother's friend to accompany them to the beach. We cannot rule out the possibility of an argument between A and B.

With or without the development of an argument, the players may come to an impasse in their interaction. In such cases, the nonperforming members of each group may be consulted for suggestions about what to say next. When a player needs help from the group, the player asks to be excused for a moment and turns to speak to the group in a low voice. Consultations should be kept brief, or else the thread of discourse may be broken.

Effects of role relationships on performances

The relationships roles have to each other affect the form of language used in interactions. How one friend speaks to another, regardless of the intentions of each, is characterized by certain aspects of language that are not found in other types of relationships. Even if they are arguing, they do it in a way that is different from the manner in which two strangers might express disagreement to each other. An obvious illustration of how language can be tailored to fit role relationships is the choice of pronouns and their accompanying verb forms in languages that provide for a grammatical distinction between familiar and formal address (e.g., German *du/Sie*, Italian *tu/Lei*, Spanish *tú/Usted*). Simply choosing a form is not enough to ensure effective interaction, however. Students need to have some awareness of the varying social constraints imposed on usage by each language. Italian and Spanish speakers generally shift from formal to familiar usage in the workplace more freely than German speakers do. Young people, especially college students, throughout Europe are more likely to use the familiar address forms among themselves than older people.

Aside from the many social constraints on language form there are also variations in word choice, idioms, intonations and style reflecting role relationships. A mother speaks to her daughter in a manner that is different from how she might speak to her professional colleagues. Long-standing business partners use language to mark their special relationship whatever the goal of the interaction might be.

It is unlikely that all the variables affecting the language used in even a limited set of role relationships could be brought out in the classroom. In fact, such an effort may not be in the best interests of the students, who can have only a limited exposure to the language. Two other goals are attainable, however, through the use of scenario performances. One goal is to assist the students in fitting the language to how they perceive themselves in the roles they are playing. Two young women arguing over the purchase of an article of clothing do not sound like two middle-aged professors disagreeing over a point of philosophy. In all probability, the students will not know how to play either kind of role in a characteristic way. The teacher should note ways in which their performances can be made more reflective of reality. The other goal is to make the students aware of the *strategic* function of socially variable language. When a speaker of Spanish invites another to *tutear*, or use the *tu* form (cf. German *duzen*, Italian *darsi del tu*, and French *tutoyer*), he or she is requesting more than a shift in grammatical usage. The invitation implies a wish to draw closer together socially and to open the discussion to subjects that are not approachable in a formal relationship. If one party continues to insist on formal address, an imbalance develops in the relationship. This imbalance may then lead to one party having a bargaining advantage. Of course, the traditional language classroom has a built-in social imbalance, since the students usually address the teacher using a title of some sort (Ms., Dr., Prof., etc.) while they, in turn, are addressed by their first names.

"Routinized" performances

Restrictions on the number of realizable goals in a conversation contributes to the "routine" effect. For example, ordering from a menu in a restaurant limits the kinds of exchanges that can take place between the customer and the waiter. The following are some likely routines in such a setting:

1. Waiter proffers menu.
2. Customer inquires about items on menu (e.g., asks what the specialty is; what the waiter recommends; whether items can be rearranged or substituted for other items).
3. Customer complains about food or delay in service.

4. Waiter offers apologies or makes excuses.
5. Customer requests check and questions charges.
6. Waiter explains charges.

The above routines exclude "small talk" that might take place between the customer and the waiter. Indeed, in some restaurants in European countries where waiters perform their roles in several languages, a switch to another topic for conversation may be beyond the waiter's language competence. But even in heavily routinized conversations there can be an interplay of strategies. The waiter may be under instructions from the chef to recommend certain dishes. The customer may have certain dietary restrictions that require an extensive rearrangement of items on the menu or a request for items not listed.

It is likely that all conversations involving public services are routinized in some way: visits to the hairdresser or barber; getting a car repaired; making purchases of various kinds, and so on. Students preparing performances on such themes should expect to follow some routines in activating their game plans.

Probably because of the medium itself, telephone conversations are marked by certain routines in most languages. The person answering the phone is expected to give some sort of signal that a line of communication has been established. Since both the caller and the respondent cannot see each other, some identification is also needed. In some cultures, the caller reserves the right to terminate the conversation. Protocols used to execute telephone routines may differ even among countries sharing the same language. In Spain, for example, one answers the phone with ¡*Dígame!* while in Mexico the expression is ¿*Bueno?* and in Puerto Rico it is *Oigo.* In some countries, respondents will state the number that has been reached by the caller. Whatever the opening protocol is, the caller will eventually ask for the identity of the respondent or request to speak with a specific person. In Italy, however, the respondent is likely to take the initiative in asking for identification: *Pronto! Chi parla?* (literally, 'Ready! Who's speaking?').

Since neither caller nor respondent can rely on facial expressions or body movements to convey attentiveness to what the other is saying, greater use is made of verbal signals throughout the telephone conversation:

"You don't say!"   (English)
"Really?"
"Uh-huh . . ."
Non me lo dici!   (Italian)
Evvero?
Sì . . .

¡No me lo digas!   (Spanish)
¿De veras?
Sí, pues . . .

When it is time to terminate a telephone conversation, English-speaking Americans often use "pre-closers" to signal the closing routine, such as the following:

"Well, it's been nice talking with you."
"I'm glad we've had this chance to talk."
"I guess I'd better get off the line."

The respondent usually acknowledges the pre-closer by saying something like:

"It was nice talking with you, too."
"Yes, it *is* getting late, isn't it?"

The caller and the respondent are then free to exchange their goodbyes and close the conversation.

   Although it would be considered impolite for the respondent to take the initiative in terminating the interaction or even use a pre-closer, he or she may try to prompt the caller into executing a pre-closer. The following would be recognized as pre-closer promptings in the United States:

"Excuse me, but someone's on the other line."
"Oh, my boss just came in and wants to talk with me."
"Sorry, but I think there's someone at the door."
"Oh, oh, my dinner is burning in the oven."

When performing scenarios in the guise of telephone conversations, students should attend to how their exchanges would be affected by the medium. In fact, it is helpful to have the students sit back-to-back so they cannot see each other, as in real telephone conversations. They should be expected to follow all routines whenever they are appropriate in target-language telephone interactions. Such routines do not detract from the strategic interplay between performers. Instead, they introduce a necessary air of authenticity to what is being transacted. Knowing what the routines are in the target language allows learners to violate them with full awareness rather than out of ignorance. Such an option should always be open in the course of instruction.

Ritualized performances

It is useful to make a distinction between routine and ritual in language performance. Whereas routines result from constraints on the variety of personal goals attainable in the interaction, ritualized performances grow from people interacting in socially defined events. Included in this category are the exchanges that occur on holidays, anniversaries, rites of passage (such as graduations and promotions), and the undertaking of new enterprises (including embarkations on long journeys). Daily social events, especially meals, are often marked by verbal rituals of various sorts. Japanese guests at mealtime, for example, should say *itadakimasu* before eating (literally, 'I take it') and *gochisosama deshita* (literally, 'It was good. I enjoyed it.') upon ending a meal. A host is likely to answer *o somatsu deshita* (literally, 'It was a poor meal'). In Japanese culture, a compliment often evokes a disclaimer by the one being complimented.

Germans have the expression *Mahlzeit* (literally, 'mealtime') to be used by a host to begin a meal. To terminate the meal, a host or even a waiter in a restaurant is likely to ask *Hat es Ihnen geschmeckt?* ('Did you like it?'), to which the guest is expected to answer in the affirmative. Among Spaniards and people from southern Italy, it is customary for someone who is eating to invite an unexpected caller to join in the home meal. A refusal would not be considered inappropriate, but it should be accompanied by an expression of gratitude for the invitation.

The place of conversational management

Although the participants in a conversation may be vying for control of it, they are bound, at least in principle, to follow what Grice (1975: 45) calls the "cooperative principle." According to this principle, participants advance the agreed-upon "purpose or direction of the talk exchange" by making their contributions as they are required. In simpler terms, we can say that conversations have a format that dictates when participants should take their turns at speech, how they should open and close a discourse, and under what circumstances they are free to change the topic under discussion. For example, opening a conversation with a stranger in Italian may be done with *Senta!* (literally, 'listen'), whereas in American English, it is likely to be achieved with an expression like "Excuse me." Topic changes can take several forms in English, for example:

"By the way..."
"Do you mind if we change the subject?"
"Not to change the subject, but..."
"That reminds me..."

A person might even attempt to carry out a topic change without bothering to announce it. In order not to give up a turn at talking, one employs a hesitation formula. In English, this formula is a mid-central unrounded vowel (sometimes written as "uh..."); the Spanish equivalent is *este...*, and in Japanese, one says the word *ano* repeatedly.

It is especially important for second-language learners to have access to those conversational management devices that are applicable when limited knowledge of the target language leads to a breakdown in communication. These devices include expressions like the following: "Sorry, I didn't understand" and "Please repeat that." To assure ready access to such expressions, some teachers print them on posters or write them on the blackboard. After the first few performances of scenarios, students seem able to employ them without being prompted.

Length of performances

No empirical studies on the optimal time span of performances have yet been done. Puhl (1984) reports that her students' performances in ESL were as brief as 1.5 minutes and as long as 12 minutes. The average, however, was around 5 minutes per performance. Probably the best answer to the question of optimal length of performance is to let the participants perform as long as they appear motivated to work toward their individual goals or until they reach an impasse. The attention span of the members of the supporting groups should also be considered. When interest begins to flag all around, it is time to terminate the performance.

Recorders in the strategic interaction classroom

Although not necessary, audio and video recorders can be helpful in the instructional process. If students are able to purchase inexpensive audio cassette recorders, they can record scenario performances for study later on. Assignments can be given that are based on recordings made in class. For example, the teacher may wish to have each student work on improving grammatical accuracy or pronunciation in a scenario. Each student may also be required to keep one cassette on which to record performances at different times during the course of instruction. In this way, an audio record is established of each student's progress in the language.

The video recorder is especially useful in the classroom because it is able to capture the nonverbal aspects of student performances. The following are some suggested uses for the video recorder:

1. taping scenarios to enhance the dramatic quality of the performance;
2. playing back recorded scenarios, pausing at various points to analyze

errors and to suggest diverse paths that could be taken in an interaction;

3. recording scenarios at different times during the semester to show students evidence of their own progress with the language;
4. using recorded scenarios to teach nonverbals, kinesics, and spatial relations conditioned by the target culture;
5. showing scenarios from other classes that might serve as models or give alternative treatments of a scenario theme;
6. playing commercially prepared videotapes.

Eventually, the availability of video equipment is likely to bring about extensive changes in the language laboratory. With the development of visual materials that are also made interactive through the programming of dialog options, the language laboratory will change from its essentially auditory nature to one in which the full range of human communication is treated.

Summary

The significance of group work becomes evident in the rehearsal phase of scenario preparation. Single roles are assigned not to individual students but to groups who collaborate in preparing them. Work groups should be kept to a size that promotes cooperation by all parties. Several scenarios can be put in rehearsal at the same time. In fact, having several scenarios in rehearsal makes it possible to keep the working groups small in size when dealing with large classes. Group work fulfills many of the goals of learner-centered instruction. It lowers the psychological barrier that might grow among some students vis-à-vis the target language. It facilitates the pooling of resources by the students and enables them to become powerful generators of knowledge. It creates a feeling of collaborative learning that is not possible in teacher-centered classrooms.

There are five specific tasks for student groups to complete during rehearsal: (1) understand the group's charge, (2) understand the ground rules, (3) explore all options open for goal achievement, (4) select someone to represent the group in the performance phase, and (5) make sure that the proper sequence of role preparation is followed. The teacher's tasks during rehearsal are to, if needed, (1) give help in forming the groups, (2) help students to uncover options for building a game plan, (3) model utterances in the target language, and (4) give focused, clear explanations of all matters requested by the students. As students approach their charge, they will reveal different "patterns" of thought. No particular pattern is to be preferred over any other, as long as it is directed to the work of the group. In addition to the need to find the strategies for realizing a goal, students will have to be made aware of cultural constraints on conversation in the target language.

Scenario performances are not for the purpose of entertaining an audience. In creating their dialogs, the student players are responsible only to themselves and the groups they represent. Performances can be typed according to how much information is shared by the players and the nature of the interaction itself. When the number of realizable goals is limited, the resulting performance is said to be routinized. When the parties involved in an interaction are expected to play out the conventions of a social event, the performance is a ritualized one. In any event, students should be made aware of the strategic function whenever possible of socially variable language use. Whatever the goals of an interaction may be, each party is expected to stay within a conversational format. To do so requires the use of management devices that signal openings, changes of topic, closings, turn-taking, and turn-keeping. Second-language learners should acquire early control over expressions that signal difficulty in understanding and request help. Mechanical aids such as cassette tape recorders and video equipment are useful in helping students to concentrate on the nature of interactive discourse throughout the course of instruction.

The contents of this chapter lead to the question of which of the two desiderata of second-language instruction – accuracy and fluency – comes first. The customary mindset is to place accuracy before fluency, motivated by the belief that students who are carefully structured in their production of well-formed sentences will ultimately expand upon this base and become fluent speakers. Perhaps the order of emphasis should be reversed, with the initial concern directed to activities that encourage students to develop fluency rather than limit them to the production of a few grammatically perfect utterances. A fluency-to-accuracy orientation entails a shift in focus away from the deconstructive process of analyzing student errors as an expression of the extent to which they have fallen short of an idealized goal of competency. Rather than accept the negative orientation of error analysis, perhaps we should direct our attention to how our students are expanding their skills in order to meet the challenge of deeper involvement in communicating through the target language.

5 Debriefing

Language teaching is a craft that rarely allows its practitioners to neglect either its art or its science. The good teacher is expected to perceive student difficulties as well as know enough about the cause of these difficulties to give the needed help. Debriefing is the phase of strategic interaction that most closely resembles the traditional activities of the language teacher: recasting in more fluent style what students have said in the target language, suggesting alternatives, leading the class in expanding upon what has been said in the target language, giving explanations and doing exercises of various types. There is, however, a critical difference between debriefing and traditional classroom work. In debriefing, the basis for all of the pedagogical elaboration is the event of the students' own performances. That is, all conscious building of student competence is from what the learners themselves have attempted to produce in the target language. In this way, the teacher facilitates the students' personal style of acquisition.

The idiosyncratic nature of acquisition was evident in a study undertaken in 1982 with seven volunteers. Included were both students and instructors brought together at two different times to determine the lasting effects of debriefing on uninitiated students. The target language was Dutch, a language unknown to any of the group. A scenario was performed (one in which the rehearsal stage was bypassed and the students were immersed directly into a dramatic situation), followed by a debriefing. During the debriefing, students were allowed to ask any questions they desired on points growing from the dialog they had created in the scenario. Some of these questions concerned vocabulary; others, pronunciation and grammar. No effort was made to follow any preordained syllabus. The second phase of the experiment took place one week later, when the group was reconvened and asked about the scenario they had performed the previous week. There was no problem in reconstructing the dialog, which was really not surprising. What was unexpected, however, was the recall of the questions *each* student had asked about the Dutch language. Not only did each remember his or her question, but each also had a perfect recall of the explanation offered by the instructor. Even more surprising was that practically no one in the group remembered anybody else's questions. What can be concluded from these observations? At the very least, we can presume that the association of conscious teaching with prior student performance is highly effective in promoting activities identified as learning ones.

Ideally, the best debriefings are organized around questions for which the students want answers. In this way, some assurance is gained that the discussion of grammar points will be received with interest by the class and will promote retention. The teacher who is accustomed to following a predetermined syllabus may wonder how there can be any assurance that all important points of grammar will be treated. Actually, this is not a serious concern in a strategic interaction class, since the significant matters of grammar will eventually surface in the course of working through scenarios.

A student-generated grammatical syllabus is preferable over one that has been composed without student input. Although teachers are traditionally concerned with covering a certain amount of material in a syllabus, there can be no easy equation between what teachers are expected to cover and what students are actually able to learn within the time span. When teachers must work with some sort of syllabus or table of contents from a textbook, the debriefings can be made to focus on targeted points of structure. In cases where there is very little opportunity for variation from a lockstep syllabus, the strategic interaction approach, with its particular way of handling structure, can be used in a supplemental way.

To the extent possible, then, the debriefing phase in strategic interaction should not be bound by what the teacher expects to cover. At the same time, there are ways for the teacher to help students chart their progress throughout the course of instruction (see, for example, the discussion on grammar logs later in this chapter). The following guidelines are offered to utilize the debriefing phase of strategic interaction to its fullest extent.

Guidelines for the teacher

(1) *Keep your priorities in order.* Debriefings should begin with commentary about the performance of the students in the scenario as a speech event. What was the outcome of the interaction? Were the intentions of the participants met? Could there have been other resolutions to the issue at hand? Only after the transactional and interactive aspects of the performance are discussed should the students' attention be drawn to issues of its structure. In this way, the primacy of function over form is maintained and the debriefing is allowed to follow a natural order of talking about speech events – that is, in the sequence of what these events were about, how they were enacted, and how the individuals involved in them played their roles. Moving on to matters of form

(grammar, vocabulary, pronunciation, and cultural conventions), it should be made evident to the students that explanations are primarily for the sake of elucidating the sample of target-language discourse and not for building a grammar that has no context in the speech event. In other words, the priority in debriefing should be the edification of target-language use within the context of live performances. One of the goals of debriefing is to encourage all students. Special care should be taken *not* to identify the particular student who made the errors being discussed, for this may discourage the learner from performing again.

(2) *Encourage students to take control of the discussion.* Students in a group tend to focus their attention on diverse aspects of the target language. Over the course of a semester, the group accumulates the resources to answer many of the questions posed by individuals within the group. By encouraging students to take the lead in the debriefing, the teacher is assured that the matters chosen for discussion are relevant to at least some members of the class. The answers that come from fellow students are also likely to be couched in terms that the questioner can readily understand and appreciate. Furthermore, questioners undergo no threat of evaluation when addressing their concerns to fellow members of the class. When the teacher dominates the question-asking process, the students may suspect that their responses are being used to evaluate their progress. As a result, an air of restraint may develop and students will refrain from inquiring about matters that are really of concern to them. Two ways to lead students to taking control of the debriefing process are:

a. Ask the class if they were able to understand each performer without difficulty. If a student admits to having difficulty, have the learner who performed repeat or paraphrase what he or she said.
b. Ask if there were some grammar points that could have caused the difficulty. Let some member of the class give the "rule" or provide a reasonable explanation.

(3) *Establish a link with past debriefings.* In order to avoid the fragmentation that can result from discussing points of grammar as discrete units, the teacher should establish links with past discussions, whenever possible. For example, inquiries about the use of a pronoun can provide the teacher with the opportunity to remind the class of other pronouns already touched upon in a past discourse. By doing so, the teacher helps the students to build a coherent grammar of the target language. It is well to keep in mind that very few elements of grammar, vocabulary, and pronunciation can be explained fully in one session. All elements of the target language are interrelated in an organic whole. To achieve the desired grammatical coherence, the teacher will need to keep track of what has been brought up from day to day. A useful way of doing

this is to keep a notebook in which entries can be made after each class, citing what points came up and in what context.

(4) *Keep explanations simple and direct.* Unhampered by the pedantry of formal grammar, students are apt to ask weighty questions in disarmingly simple words: for example, "Why is it *un chapeau blanc* and not *un blanc chapeau?*" The teacher may find it hard to resist the temptation of giving a lengthy explanation of adjective placement in French. Grammatical rules about this topic range from the very general ones about the French preference for postpositioning adjectives to the finer-grained rules concerning specific kinds of adjectives (size, color, and so on). Teachers who survive year after year of hearing this question are apt to arm themselves with rules about adjectives that cover the entire field. But what to tell this particular student in this particular situation? What motivated the question? Did it grow from ignorance about the general placement of adjectives, or was it a more specific concern about how to emphasize that the hat was white and not blue or red? The teacher should try to remember the context of the phrase in question in order to decide how to answer the question. Perhaps it will be sufficient in this case to tell the student that adjectives generally come after the nouns they modify in French. It may be difficult for the student to take in more than this general statement. On the other hand, the need might exist for the teacher to go into the matter of adjective displacement to express special emphasis: *un blanc chapeau,* that is, *white* hat (and not a red one). Whatever the case, the general procedure should be to give the student enough information to be satisfied with the answer and not be confused by details that may only give rise to more questions.[1]

Such a case was evident in a Spanish class I visited. A student had been playing the role of a hostess entreating another student (acting as a dinner guest) to eat a rather suspect meal of eels. The hostess vacillated between saying ¡*Cóme!* and ¡*Cóma!* It was inevitable that this student would take advantage of the debriefing phase to ask what form should have been used. Rather than try to determine the motivation for the student's question, the instructor launched into a detailed explanation of the subjunctive mood in Spanish and how some forms of it are used to express polite commands. He lined up the paradigms of several verbs on the blackboard, taking care to point out how verbs of the second and third conjugations use a final *-a* for polite commands and an *-e* for familiar ones while verbs of the first conjugation do just the opposite. The student sat politely and silently through the entire presentation. As

---

1 Schachter (1983) supports the notion that individual students may differ in how much input they need to set their language acquisition devices into motion. By allowing questions to develop naturally and then providing answers that do not ramble, the teacher is apt to meet the students' particular needs for input.

the hostess filed out at the end of the class period, I heard her mutter to a fellow student, "I still would like to know what I should have said."

Evidently, this particular student's concern was an interactive one involving what form would be polite yet friendly to her guest. To uncover this concern, the instructor should have asked how she viewed her relationship to the guest. Did she feel older and authoritarian, or was she trying to achieve a feeling of intimacy that comes with peers? It may have been sufficient for the teacher to recommend the form *¡Cóme!* in the latter case or *¡Cóma!* in the former one, saving the details of verb morphology for some other time. The irony of this episode was that the student did not get the explanation she wanted and was probably more confused now. The instructor, however, felt that he had done justice to the issue. In his view, he had been able to use one student's inquiry about an important grammatical matter to launch into a thorough presentation of it for the entire class.

It is useful to distinguish between grammar and metalinguistic activities in the classroom. There is no real evidence that teaching grammar as a self-contained system representing vital knowledge of the target language has any effect on developing either accuracy or fluency in using the language. Yet there is ample evidence to show that people believe this to be the case. Students who are literate in their own languages expect to be made literate in the new one they are studying. They expect to be able to talk about its rules, to prove their competence to others who believe as they do. Elgin (1980) thinks of grammatical rules as "incantations" that call up skills from the inner reaches of competence. Students from a traditional German class at the University of Delaware were observed to hesitate in their first-time performance of a scenario, sometimes in the middle of a sentence, and look to the teacher or to other students for help, saying "subordinate clause" and "dative case." Their grammatical training had made them aware of the form of what they were trying to say but did not help them say it.

Some guidelines for students

It is helpful to inform the learners about some basic procedures in debriefing. Not much detail needs to be given because the full significance of these procedures will become clearer with each new debriefing conducted over the course of instruction.

(1) *Feel free to ask or comment about anything relating to the target language or its use.* It may be that something said by a scenario participant was confusing to a classmate observing the performance. Perhaps a certain expression triggered several questions about the use of a verb or the form of a noun. On some occasions, the matter of concern to the

91

student may appear to have no obvious connection to the discourse of the scenario. No matter. If the question results from a concern of the student, then it should be asked, with the expectation that the teacher will try to answer it. The underlying principle here is that the purposes of instruction are best served when the teacher provides explanations that the students really want to have. In order for debriefings to be maximally effective, students need to feel that their concerns will be met as quickly and directly as possible.

(2) *Be tolerant of the teacher.* Students should realize that every instructor has limitations. These limitations may include lacunae in several areas of the target language. No one, not even a so-called native speaker, can know everything about a language. If the teacher cannot supply answers to all questions on demand, students should be willing to accept a "promissory note" that the teacher will do some research and provide answers at the next class meeting. Students should not be surprised if some of their questions are hard to answer. Difficult questions are tangible landmarks along the pathway of developing competencies. The teacher who respects the students' questions, despite the inability to answer them, does not suffer a loss of status as the prime knower and main guide to competency. Novice teachers will discern a pattern of questions developing over the times that the same course is conducted. Eventually, the seemingly unanswerable questions will become answerable and dwindle in number. A good suggestion for students is to write the difficult questions on slips of paper, to be collected at the end of the class session. In this way, the teacher will have a written record of what was asked and the students will be reassured that their questions will be answered eventually.

(3) *Do not be afraid to make mistakes.* Students should be aware that accuracy grows with practice. The more one speaks or writes, the better one becomes at these activities. The debriefing phase – especially if it is conducted in the target language – is not a time for the teacher to evaluate how well the students are speaking. Of course, accuracy in the use of the target language is as important as gaining fluency in it. However, it is within the matrix of fluent speech that accuracy eventually develops.

Contextualizing grammar

Accepting the importance of contextualizing grammar is not enough. Many textbooks already contextualize grammar by presenting grammar points in the format of contrived conversations and dialogs. The preferred way to contextualize grammar in an interactive methodology is to start with utterances taken from the students' own performances and then associate grammar to these performances as needed by the students. For example, if an EFL/ESL student produces the following:

"I want to buy the car."

when first approaching a classmate playing the part of a car dealer, the teacher can contrast it with

"I want to buy a car."

in which the indefinite article is correctly used in this context. The two sentences can serve as reference points to help the student understand how the indefinite article in English functions in sentences where no information is shared with the addressee about its antecedent. Once a point of reference is established (*a* car, in this case), then the two speakers can start using the definite article (e.g., "How much do you want to pay for the car?"). Actually, the label "indefinite" is a poor one, since the speaker may have in mind a particular make of car or may have already decided upon one of the cars being sold by the dealer. Titles given grammatical elements are often misleading in this way. The teacher should try to make the explanation reflect the function of the grammatical item rather than fit the title given to it.

Another way to contextualize grammar is to let the students experience the results of their own errors in discourse. An illustration of this technique comes from a class in Spanish taught at the high school level (S-J. DiLaura Morris, personal communication). In this particular instance, a student incorrectly used the third-person pronoun instead of the second-person form. Expressing a desire to begin a conversation with a classmate, he said:

¿Cómo se llama? ('What is her name?')

instead of

¿Cómo te llamas tú? ('What is your name?')

The teacher allowed the intended addressee to play through the scenario as if she had been asked for information about someone else. The significance of the incorrect pronoun was eventually felt by the student as he came to realize that it misdirected his efforts at conversation.

Keeping a grammar log

The grammar log is a device that allows students to satisfy their desire for formal grammatical work while assuring that grammar will serve some real purpose in the learning process. In operation, the grammar log is a running account made by students of points about the target language that each perceives as significant. The log is filled out as part of the debriefing process or as a result of it. The instructor informs the students that they may write whatever they wish in their logs about any component of the language that strikes them as salient to the day's work. To help students organize their logs, an outline like the following may be supplied to them:

LESSON HIGHLIGHTS   NAME _____

DATE _____

1. *Vocabulary and idioms*
   Write here as many of the new words as you can remember from today's lesson:

   _____

   _____

   _____

2. *Structures*
   Note examples of new constructions learned today. Include brief statements about the grammar points they illustrate:

   _____

   _____

   _____

3. *Conversational strategies*
   What new expressions did you learn today?
   What goals did these expressions accomplish?

   _____

   _____

   _____

4. *Matters that need more work*
   Note here in brief form any points you are still having trouble understanding:

   _____

   _____

In order to assure the students that these logs will be taken seriously, the teacher should announce that every student's log will be examined periodically. It must be made clear, however, that the logs are personal interpretations of what was learned each day and they are not expected to be uniform for the entire class. What is expected is an indication that each student is taking note of his or her own difficulties and is trying to do something about them. Grammar, from this perspective, becomes an output of the instructional process, rather than an input. It allows each student to attend to matters as they occur. Observations are made from the discourse generated in the scenarios and the explanations given during the debriefing sessions. In this way, entries in the log are guaranteed to be more focused and useful.

The grammar log, or any device similar to it used in connection with the debriefing phase, reaffirms the seriousness of the instructional program. Students conditioned to objectifying what they are learning need to engage in an activity that is identified traditionally with the subject matter. Scenario work reduces the anxiety that sometimes comes with second-language learning, but this reduction should not be at the price of a disorientation resulting from no requirement to display tokens of learning. In a high school or college curriculum that includes courses in history, mathematics, and science, the language program that does not include grammar work of some kind may suffer from a loss of status in the minds of students.

The place of grammar

The perception that grammar is important regardless of its relevance is apparently shared by many. In a survey conducted at the University of Delaware in 1983, I asked the foreign-language students point-blank what grammar meant to them. One of the most revealing answers obtained from this survey was: "Grammar is a way to know that you have learned something about the language you are studying." The belief that grammar somehow embodies all that is crucial to the target language was evident even in conversational classes at the same university. Students entering these classes from traditional audiolingual ones at the lower level sometimes expressed the fear that they were not progressing because they were not given explicit grammar drills and exercises. The same need for grammar was found by Morris (1987) at the high school level. On the other hand, the same author (see DiLaura 1983) found that agricultural scientists were able to proceed well without a grammar base in a course in Spanish that dovetailed with intermittent trips to Spanish-speaking countries. Apparently, the time spent being surrounded by Spanish speakers kept the scientists aware of the importance of interactive skills over grammatical knowledge in their study of Spanish.

It is difficult to resist the temptation in the classroom to manipulate

95

student conversation so that it highlights structures and vocabulary that the teacher considers to be important. The following are two well-known manipulations:

1. Refusing to respond to anything students might say, even correctly, in the target language that has not been presented as part of the lesson for the day. *No es la pregunta para hoy* ('That's not the question for today') is a verbal strategy often used to discourage students from expressing themselves freely.
2. Patterning the conversation so that students must use the forms that are the topics for the day, as in *¿Dónde está el Paseo de la Reforma?* ('Where's the Paseo de la Reforma?'). If the student answers *en México* ('in Mexico'), which is factually as well as grammatically correct, the answer is not accepted and the student is made to repeat after the teacher: *Está en México* ('It is in Mexico').

These ploys have the effect of focusing the students' attention on the form of what they are trying to say rather than on the purpose for communication. The teacher who manipulates student conversation in this way is employing the target language as an illustration of itself rather than as a conveyor of meaning.

Hartwell (1985) contains an extensive treatment of the place of grammar in language instruction. One of Hartwell's points is that the experiments done with grammar give results that are not easily interpreted. For example, the improvement shown by students in syntax after having had instruction in transformational grammar may be more the result of having engaged in active manipulation of language than the learning of a particular model of grammar. It seems that some instructors think that students learn only what they are taught and will not learn otherwise.

It is difficult to generalize about the place of formal grammatical instruction in the classroom. Students who have been exposed to it as a part of their general education are likely to expect it to be a part of their instructional program in a new language. The actual contribution grammar makes to the learning of the new language, however, is open to question. According to a study conducted by Seliger (1983), only nine of fifty-five native and second-language respondents were able to provide a rule for how they chose between the two forms "a" and "an" of the indefinite article in English. No relationship was found to exist between these students' ability to state the rule – correctly or incorrectly – and the competence to perform it appropriately.

What can we conclude from this discussion? Grammar will most likely remain a part of our tradition of second-language instruction. It appears to answer a need felt by many learners to objectify knowledge about the target language. Just how knowledge about a language relates to what really helps learners to speak and understand that language is a matter that is open for much more psycholinguistic investigation. The important task in the classroom is to determine the extent to which explicit reference to grammar enhances the debriefing phase for each group of learners. The grammar log has been suggested as being useful in this respect. Some classes may like it very much. Others may not respond favorably to it, especially those who do not come from a tradition of grammar-oriented instruction. Whatever the case, the most appropriate way to view all conscious grammatical treatment in student-centered, interactive classes is as output from the students. Its explanatory power is relative to how well each learner has been able to understand the samples of actual discourse experienced throughout the course of instruction.

How to identify the best learners

According to Rubin and Thompson (1982), the best learners share several traits. They are willing to ask questions (certainly desirable for successful debriefing). They also try to generalize from the explanations and examples given to them (another desirable trait). In general, they are the students who show the most involvement in the work of the classroom.

How can Rubin and Thompson's observations be interpreted within the context of the strategic interaction approach? Almost every class is likely to contain students who are chatty and eager to verbalize. Although such students are often very good learners, others who are less vocal and prefer to take notes and listen quietly have equally legitimate learning styles. The successful debriefing phase provides the opportunity for many learning styles to be activated. The students who listen while others dominate the discussion may be profiting greatly from being passive. Ultimately, the success of the learner is revealed in how well he or she interacts with others through the target language. The effectiveness of debriefing, as well as that of rehearsal, is assessed in terms of subsequent performances. Any other measure is only incidental.

Summary

Debriefing is the third of the three phases of strategic interaction. Although the debriefing activity resembles traditional second-language teaching through its exchange of questions and answers about the target language, it differs markedly from customary classroom practice in the way grammar is approached and in the initial focus on interaction. The view of grammar as the organizing element in second-language learning is seriously questioned in this chapter. There is no clear evidence that students apply explicit grammatical knowledge to the improvement of performances. On the other hand, there is reason to believe that second-language students may achieve competence by receiving explanations of grammatical matters in answer to their own felt needs. Grammar is more appropriately viewed as output than as input in an interactive approach. By attending to the ways in which students talk about the structure of the target language and formulate their own explanations, the teacher can gain an insight into their progress. A useful aid to creating grammatical output is the "grammar log," in which students keep a lesson-by-lesson record of what has come to their attention in the target language.

Several guidelines are provided for both the teacher and the students to facilitate the work of the debriefing session. Basically, these guidelines foster student-initiated inquiries and commentary about the performances on which the debriefings are organized. The teacher may start the debriefing by asking about the theme and outcome of the scenario performance. The general emphasis is placed on how well the scenario performers attained their goals. Specific errors are not used to chastise the individuals who made them. Students should not be hesitant to make mistakes but should attempt to be as fluent as possible. Accuracy comes with practice. Finally, debriefing is not an occasion to evaluate students. Evidence of successful learning is to be found in improved performances in subsequent scenarios.

6 Building literacy on an interactive base

In the strategic interaction classroom, the skills of reading and writing ideally begin with the performance of scenarios. The belief is that learners develop a strong foundation for literacy in the target language when they can derive the practice of writing from their own active participation in spoken discourse. This belief leads to concentration first on the creation of texts and to an interpretation of reading as a skill that depends greatly on understanding the context of written passages. Therefore, suggestions for reading exercises are to be found in the next chapter, where they can be developed with regard to literature. The fundamentals of writing will occupy most of our attention here.

Phelps (1985) documents a change in the meaning of the term "process" as it relates to writing. Where "process" once referred only to the writer's creation of the text, it is now commonly extended to include the activity of the readers as they construct meanings from the text. According to Phelps, this shift in meaning leads toward a more "intersubjective and deeply contextualized view of written language" (1985: 14). While this expanded interpretation of how meaning grows from texts is welcome, we must place it in our particular circumstances, in which nonnative learners are writing for readers (fellow learners) who are also nonnative. By basing writing tasks on episodes (such as scenarios), writers and readers are given a source from which to draw shared knowledge. This shared knowledge helps to build coherence into the texts produced by the students. In a sense, the classroom generates its own culture. In the case of students who come from diverse cultures, classroom culture is the only one they share and cooperate in as equals. The potential benefit of classroom culture should not be overlooked in generating texts. Nor should we overlook another characteristic of ESL, EFL, and FL classes alike, namely that they provide perhaps the only opportunity students have in an educational setting to express personal judgments on a wide range of human concerns. The creation of texts that are then shared with others about such concerns is an educational experience of intrinsic value beyond that of language-learning. No student comes away from a successful language-learning experience without growing inward as well as outward.

Literacy remains under much discussion by theorists these days, and we are just beginning to understand the complexity of creating and comprehending texts. The following observations about literacy form the background for the strategic interaction approach to the subject:

(1) Literacy cannot be measured in absolute terms. Literate users of a language do not necessarily possess a broad command of reading and writing in the language (see Heath 1983; Frawley 1987). It is unrealistic to expect learners to acquire more literacy than natives generally have.

Literacy is best described as a continuum, with individual members of society arrayed at different points on the continuum as reflected in what they read and how they read it (Frawley 1987). If such an interpretation of literacy in society is correct – and it appears to be well-founded in reality – what kind of skill in reading and writing should second-language learners acquire? The immediate answer to this question is not to expect them all to gain equal levels of competence. Each student is probably best evaluated in terms of specific reading and writing tasks, such as reporting and commenting. It is to be expected that students will display differing degrees of achievement in each task, since even regular users of the target language vary in their abilities to write and to read various materials. To evaluate fairly, the teacher can take the overall achievement of each student as it matches one of several acceptable types of customary performance. If regular users are not alike in their command of writing and reading, why should we expect second-language learners to conform to some hypothetical norm?

(2) The state of literacy involves the principle of self-regulation. Following Lantolf and Frawley (1983), strategic interaction adopts the Vygotskyan perspective which recognizes that learners must pass through three kinds of regulation to achieve literacy: *object*-regulation (with the writing conventions of the language controlling the output of the writer), *other*-regulation (control of the writer by others, such as the teacher), and *self*-regulation (achieved when the writer assumes control over his or her output).

(3) The background knowledge of readers influences their comprehension of what is contained within the text. Texts with a high content of target culture can be especially difficult for language learners (see Johnson 1982; Carrell and Eisterhold 1983; Quinn 1984). Teachers should anticipate the kinds of interpretation students are likely to give when reading texts in the target language.

(4) The structural arrangement of information in a text as well as the rhetorical devices used by the writer are to be considered. McCreary (1984) has demonstrated how considerable the difference may be in rhetorical styles and discourse organization between Japanese and North American business transactions.

(5) Written texts are more detached from their original contexts and

are more internally coherent than their spoken counterparts. To create written versions of spoken discourse (such as reports, stories, essays), literate people apply conventions that allow their writing to be removed from its original context in the speech act without becoming incoherent (see Redeken 1984).

(6) Monologic texts are further removed from spoken language performance than are dialogic texts. Following Vygotsky (1962), it is dialog, with its turn-taking and other features of conversational management, that provides the opportunity for all three kinds of regulation (object, other, and self) to operate. The monolog-type text need not be so heavily loaded with strategic rhetoric if the writer's main purpose is to be expository rather than persuasive. Monologs are more difficult to write than dialogs (see further discussion under "Dialog Writing" later in this chapter). In order to be coherent, free-standing texts with the expectation of being understood by an unseen readership, monologs must follow conventions imposed on them by the target culture. Student writers of monolog-type essays or reports must decide on how much background information to include, where to put it, and how to express it in a language that is not native to them. An effort to minimize the difficulties of making such decisions is found in foreign-language teaching materials that contain basic writing and reading exercises such as fill-ins. For example, Krashen and Terrell (1983) provide a chart to fill in with the personal characteristics of students in the class (e.g., eye color: ____, clothes worn: ____). Uncaptioned cartoons are another device used to control structural limitations in writing.

Dalbuono-Glassman and Bosco (1982) follow yet another approach to literacy in the target language. In their textbook for advanced students of Italian (*Profili*), they provide a series of narratives (such as descriptions of individuals) to which students are asked to react in various ways. For example, Franco is a lover of opera and Maria, a rock enthusiast. The assignment may be to prepare a dialog between the two on the subject of music.

(7) Written texts must be both cohesive and coherent. According to Halliday and Hasan (1976), the linguistic ties between elements within a text make it cohesive. Coherence, however, involves the context of the text and the information shared by the writer and the reader (see also Carrell 1982). This research on written texts points up the need for language teachers to address several questions: What makes our students' compositions coherent as well as cohesive? What guidelines shall we give them? It appears that the mechanics of cohesion are more easily taught, since the devices that make a text cohesive are usually elements of grammar.

Three tasks in the achievement of literacy

What are the steps that lead toward the kind of writing and reading skills needed by large numbers of people living and working in the literate societies of the world?

1: Supplying factual information in a predetermined format

We start with a discourse that the students have generated. It may be a discourse built around an automobile accident. Perhaps the persons involved in it were two drivers and a police officer. We can imagine the course of events as follows:

> A is hurrying to keep an important appointment with her attorney. As she turns left at a busy intersection, her car is struck on its right side by another vehicle driven by B. B is on his way to meet his boss, who is impatiently waiting at the airport. In the ensuing exchange between A and B, each blames the other for the accident. A insists that the traffic light was in her favor, indicating permission to turn left. B claims that the traffic light had already changed and allowed him to continue through the intersection. As the confrontation continues, a police officer arrives to investigate.

In real life, reports are often required by law after an accident takes place. Their format is likely to include a pictorial representation of the accident, accompanied by answers to questions and a brief narrative describing what happened. If possible, the teacher should obtain a copy of an authentic accident report form. In the absence of such a form, the teacher can prepare an imitation one, with a block in which to draw the picture, a set of questions to answer, and a place for the narrative (see Figure 6.1).

The accident report may be assigned as homework. Once the students have completed them, the teacher may distribute the ones filled out by role A workers to those who prepared role B, and vice versa. Students can be asked to read each other's reports and comment on their accuracy in setting forth the "facts" of the accident. Another step can be to set up a panel of judges comprised of students who do not take part in the scenario to rule on who, if anyone, was right. Debriefing periods can be given over to discussing problems of grammar, word choice, and style.

2: Writing with more self-regulation

Literacy comes in degrees of increasing control over the mechanisms of the writing process. Filling out an accident report is largely a task regulated by the formal structure imposed upon the learner by outside

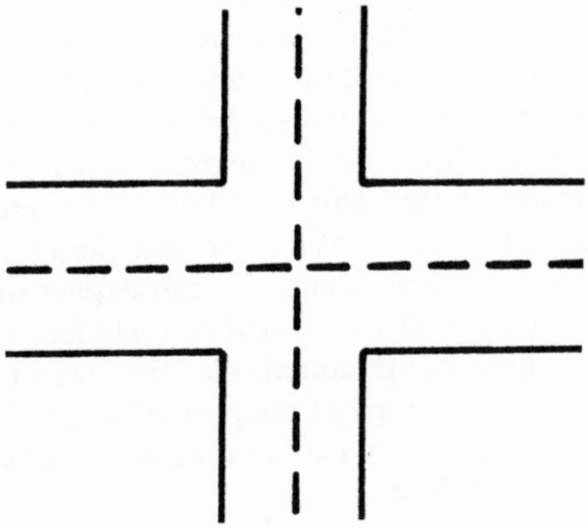

When you draw the picture, use rectangles (▭) to represent the vehicles and mark yours with an X (☒).

Draw an arrow in the upper left-hand corner to indicate North.

Position vehicles at the point of impact.

Questions to answer:

1. What time of day did the accident occur?

   ____

2. What were the weather conditions?

   ____

3. How fast were you going?

   ____

In your own words, describe the events of the accident as you remember them:

____

____

____

____

____

Figure 6.1. Accident report

forces. Little choice is given to the writer of the report on how facts are to be arranged. There is also little opportunity to represent personal opinions and attitudes. The format of the task regulates how the writer creates the text and subsequently how it is interpreted by the reader. In exchange for this lack of freedom in self-expression is the assurance that the resulting text will be coherent, with its parts arranged cohesively. Once the students have had this experience, however, they are ready to move on to acquiring more personal control over writing (and reading) in the target language. Writing a news account of a public event like an accident occupies an intermediate position on the students' way to self-regulation. Newspaper articles may reflect varying degrees of personal opinion, but they generally purport to represent the "facts" of events. To capitalize on the nature of newspaper writing, we can direct the students to compose an article about the accident. We can expect that the facts (i.e., what, how, where, why, and when) will be included, but we will also allow the freedom to give an opinion about some aspect of the accident, such as placing the blame on one of the parties or labeling the intersection a dangerous one and therefore exonerating both parties. Two such sample newspaper articles follow:

Sample newspaper articles

A man rushing to the airport was unable to avoid colliding with a car that turned into his path at the intersection of Maple Avenue and Main Street. The accident happened yesterday at 6 P.M. The driver of the other car was a young woman. She was making a left turn when struck. The other party in the accident insisted that the traffic light had changed and actually gave him the right of way. The police officer who investigated the accident issued a ticket to the man for reckless driving.

The busy intersection of Maple Avenue and Main Street has been the scene of yet another accident. Yesterday at 6 P.M., a man proceeding south on Maple Street to the airport collided with a young woman who was making a left turn onto Main. The police officer who investigated the accident refused to issue any tickets to the parties involved. He said that the intersection was a dangerous one and that it was impossible to identify anyone as the guilty party.

As with the accident reports, students may be asked to read each other's newspaper articles and then comment on how they were organized.

3: Writing for an intimate readership

The pathway to full self-regulation in writing ultimately leads to the composing of personal letters. Again, the episode of the automobile accident can serve as the basis for writing. The assignment to the students can be to write a letter to a friend about the accident. The letter can be from the point of view of one of the parties involved in it or as an onlooker. Here is a sample:

Dear Daddy,

How have you been? I hope that your rheumatism hasn't been bothering you recently. Do you remember the nice red car you bought me? Well, it's been totaled in an accident. Don't worry about me. I wasn't hurt. Also, the insurance company will pay for most of the cost of replacing it. The next time I drive home it will be in a new blue car that I'm thinking of buying.

          Love,

_____

The above is written in what has been called "intimate style." Interestingly enough, it resembles one half of a two-way conversation, with the writer anticipating what the other party might say (e.g., "Don't worry about me"). An onlooker might write something like the following:

Dear Mom,

Did you read in the paper about the accident at Maple and Main? Well, I was there. It was spectacular but no one got hurt. Driving in this city can be dangerous. I'm glad I don't have to worry about owning a car. I'll be home for the weekend.

         Love,

_____

Dialog writing

The linguistic creativity of learners can be tapped in a special way by having them write dialogs in the format of scenario performances. Since such dialogs are supposed to represent spoken discourse, dialog writers are relieved of the need to adhere to the conventions of expository composition in the target language. There are several ways to conduct this type of exercise:

(1) Have the role players and their supporting groups collaborate in producing a written version of their interaction. This activity could also be assigned as homework to individual students, following a debriefing of the spoken performance in class.

(2) Ask the students to produce a written dialog that follows a line of development that is different from the one taken in the spoken performance. In this way, students can draw from the pool of unused strategies that they prepared during the rehearsal phase.

(3) Instruct the nonperforming members of the class to write out the dialog as they remember it from the spoken performance. In preparation for this, the teacher may lead the class in making a list of the words and expressions that seemed most strategically important in the spoken version of the dialog. The list serves as reminders of the general flow of conversation.

(4) Have the students prepare their dialogs from written descriptions of situations derived from scenarios. The following is an example based on a scenario developed by Julie Docker of the Australian National University in Canberra:

Original Scenario: Journey to the Past

Role A: You are traveling on a train and are sitting next to someone who looks familiar to you. This person appears to be the one who once sold you an expensive TV set that stopped working after one week. You were unable to complain to this person because when you returned to the store he/she was no longer there. What will you say now?

Role B: You work as a traveling salesperson and you are riding on a train next to a very well-dressed person. Since you sell clothing, this person might be interested in some of your merchandise or may even be in the clothing business. What will you say to him/her?

Derived situation supplied to the students: Two strangers find themselves riding together on a train. One of them decides that the other resembles a salesperson who sold him/her a defective TV set at some time in the past. The other insists that he/she sells clothing. Develop a dialog that might occur between them.

In one classroom application of this scenario, A tried a number of strategies, asking first if B ever sold TV sets, then suggesting that B might have a twin in the TV business, and finally offering to buy some clothes in B's store, if B would admit to having sold A a defective TV set. B countered A's accusations and insinuations first by denying any connection with TVs and radios, and then by attempting to change the subject. The change of subject took the form of a compliment to A's appearance. Neither party gave ground, and the interaction ended in an impasse. The inherent liveliness of this scenario (arising to a large extent from the 'mistaken identity' theme) makes it appealing to inventive dialog writers.

The activities outlined in this chapter are intended only as illustrations of how learners can be guided toward literacy in the target language. The examples of filling out reports, composing newspaper articles, writing personal letters, and preparing dialogs are not intended to be exclusive guideposts in the process. It is the task of the teacher (or curriculum planner, as the case may be) to determine what kinds of writing and reading skills are most appropriate to literate functioning in the target culture. Whatever these may be, the orientation proceeds from spoken interactions to writing that stands at increasing distances from the context of speech.

Correcting the written homework assignment

It would be inappropriate to end a chapter on reading and writing in the classroom without making some remarks about correcting homework assignments. Getting back an assignment that has red pencil marks all over it can be devastating for a student. Semke (1984) warns against overcorrecting. There is evidence that corrections may not increase writing accuracy and, in fact, may even have a negative effect on student attitudes. According to Semke, correction should be selective. It should be done in a way to help move the students toward increased accuracy by focusing their attention on matters of global significance.

This view of correction parallels the one put forth for debriefing procedures in the classroom. In correcting assignments done at home, the teacher should not leave the student feeling helpless about the writing task. To be sure, correction is more an art than a science. However it is carried out, the emphasis should fall on how much the writer has been able to master rather than on how much further the writer has to go.

Summary

Writing is placed before reading in the strategic interaction approach to literacy. This particular order helps learners to proceed through steps that lead ultimately to the kind of control over texts that habitual users of the language have. We still have much to learn about the nature of reading and writing. So far, researchers have suggested that literacy cannot be measured in absolute terms, that the structure of a text is affected by cultural conventions, and that written texts are more detached from their original contexts than spoken ones. Monologic texts are likely to be more difficult for learners than dialogic ones because the former are more removed from their origins in discourse than the latter. An important factor in making written texts coherent depends on how well they reflect their context and manage their informational content. Three tasks are proposed for the achievement of literacy in the target language: Put factual information in a predetermined format; write with increasing self-regulation; and achieve the ability to write for intimate readerships.

7 Strategic interaction in the teaching of literature

It is customary in second-language education to think of instruction as having two tiers. The first tier is dedicated to achieving the basics. The second tier is the one in which the focus of instruction shifts to the so-called content areas. To illustrate these two tiers we can cite the presence of special ESL institutes at American universities where foreign students enroll in order to acquire a basic competence in English. Courses in such institutes normally do not carry college credit. The students enrolled in them are not usually matriculated in the regular academic programs of the university. A similar arrangement is made in American schools for elementary-level children who are not proficient in English. These children are given special classes in ESL with the hope of eventually mainstreaming them with English-speaking children in the regular classes. In foreign-language education, students cannot usually gain access to second-tier courses until they have either gone through the prerequisite lower-level "skill" courses or have demonstrated that they do not need such instruction.

A wide gap exists between first-tier "skill" courses and second-tier "content" courses from the perspective of both students and teachers. Students who perform well in traditional skill courses may not excel in the content courses that follow. EFL teachers in non-English-speaking countries often complain that methodologists develop new approaches primarily for the basic level. The methodology used for literature is largely unchanged from the traditional lecture type of the second tier. Foreign-language courses dealing with literary subjects in the United States often make no allowances for language-learning problems. It is assumed by many who teach literature that students at this level already know the target language and that the "skill-getting" process has been completed. The extent to which this assumption is valid is unknown. Anecdotal evidence obtained from literature teachers and students alike indicates that a considerable amount of first-tier work is needed even in the advanced literature courses.

The disparity between the two tiers of courses suggests that:

1. teaching content in the target language is not realistically a procedure that can be postponed until students acquire the so-called basic skills in the language;

2. given the learners' need to continue acquiring skills through the second tier, the approach to be used in advanced courses should proceed logically from the previous instructional experience of the students.

In other words, no great gap need separate skill and content courses. In fact, a strategic interaction approach to second-language instruction provides for a gradual and smooth transition from beginning to advanced-level courses. The purpose of this chapter is to outline the ways in which the teaching of target-language literature can utilize strategic interaction.

Literature was selected as the subject of this chapter over a number of other possible content areas (e.g., history or art) for several reasons. In the traditional program of language instruction, literature is considered the principal subject matter for advanced courses. In North American universities, the great majority of upper-level courses in foreign-language departments are dedicated to literary studies. People who pursue formal study of a foreign language beyond the basic skill courses are expected to know something about the body of literature written in that language. Knowing what literate natives read and discuss among themselves is very helpful to the learner who wishes to share in the valued products of the target culture. Probably the most important reason for selecting literature, however, is the great need felt by teachers for a better understanding of how to teach literature to readers who are not also native speakers of the target language. No nation ever created a literature for readers who are not also speakers of its language. This fact alone makes it essential that foreign-language teachers consider instruction in literature to be an extended exercise in exposing learners to the language and its uses.

The appreciation of literature

We commonly use the term "appreciation" to define the state of getting a reaction to the reading of literary texts that goes beyond pure enjoyment. The reader who "appreciates" literature can somehow relate it to the canons of a genre or a stylistic period. The problem is that such appreciation by the learner is not easily achieved. In an experiment done with American students of German, Bernhardt (1985) found that her subjects did not naturally appreciate the special literary nature of the texts they were reading. Only one provided a translation into English that reflected the special literary genre of the original German text, albeit in a crude way. De Beaugrande (1984) explains the process of literary analysis as transforming the linearly ordered information on a page into a hierarchical format. In each literate tradition there are special conventions for ordering information so that it fits the accepted genres. To get second-language learners to an understanding of these conventions is a major task in the teaching of literature.

The Vygotskyan perspective

In the relationship between the student-reader and the piece of literature we find reflected, once again, the three kinds of regulation (object, other, and self) that were applied to gaining literacy in second languages in Chapter 6. For students who are struggling with the language itself, the experience of reading the piece does not go beyond object-regulation. The text presents linguistic problems that occupy most of the students' attention. Under such circumstances, no progress can be made toward the other types of regulation. Object-regulated students look up many words and write translations in the margins or over the tops of the words. They miss the clues that make the text cohesive, such as the placement of pronouns and conjunctions.

Other-regulated students are in sufficient control of the mechanics of the text to be able to respond to the teacher's commentaries and judgments of it as literature. Other-regulation usually takes up much of the class time in traditional literature courses. When it is properly done, students are finally led to self-regulation. When it is improperly done, the process is stalled and the result is what Lantolf (1984), following Freire, calls "oppression." The characteristics of oppression are found in those teachers who insist on lockstep answers to questions and accept no deviance from the analysis they impose on the text. In such cases, students are unlikely to relate the piece to their own experience or interpretations.

Self-regulation is gained when the reader is able to evaluate the work in terms of his or her own opinion and then come to a personal conclusion about the work's extended meaning and its effect on the reader.

The literary text as discourse

A poster put up in the heat of a political campaign exhorting all to vote a certain candidate into office has a clear discourse value. Whether one accepts its particular message or not, the poster is functioning in an interaction with all those who see it. Taken down after the elections and relegated to the scrap heap or to someone's collection of political memorabilia, the poster becomes a mere token text. The most significant aspect of texts is not their structure but their participation in dialogues that people share with each other. Literary texts are committed to this interactive participation to an extent far greater than posters and other public signs; thus we should be able to find that same value in reading them.[1] Burke (1973: 296) called texts "strategies for dealing with situations"; McClosky (1984: 386) would redefine "the often passive activity of reading" as a "strenuous act." Paving the way to reader involvement with the text, McKay (1982) proposes that students be asked what they would have done if they had been one of the characters in the stories they are reading. If literary texts are to take their rightful place in vivid human discourse, then the reader must undergo some of the same creative processes experienced by the writer.[2] Consider the following:

> You have been transported back to the nineteenth century. You find yourself riding in a carriage together with other refugees from the Franco-Prussian War. In your haste, you were unable to bring along any food. Only one other passenger had the foresight to bring along a basket of bread, cheese, and fruit. You note that your fellow passengers have shunned this woman because she is a prostitute. What will you do? Will you befriend her and ask her to share her food with you?

We can make the scene even more interesting:

> The carriage is forced to stop at an inspection point manned by unfriendly Prussian soldiers. They are hesitant to let you and your fellow travelers pass. The officer in charge takes an interest in the prostitute and offers to let the carriage pass in exchange for her services. She is very patriotic, however, and refuses to yield to the soldier. Do you join the other passengers in attempting to convince her that she should appease him?

Does the latter situation sound familiar? It was taken from *Boule de suif* by Guy de Maupassant (I am indebted to Professor Mary Donaldson-Evans of the University of Delaware for this example). Maupassant provides a biting social commentary on the passengers in the carriage, showing them to be hypocritical in their attitudes toward the prostitute.

1 The views of literary analyst M. M. Bakhtin (1981) are largely compatible with the approach to literature taken in this chapter. According to Bakhtin, there are many voices to be heard in a piece of creative literature. The reader chooses among these voices within the specific set of circumstances of each act of reading. Bakhtin argues convincingly that dialog lies at the heart of all human creativity with language.

2 Authors are aware of the discoursive nature of their texts and sometimes engage in vigorous literary exercises to prove the point. A lively literary discourse is found in *The Floating Admiral*, a mystery written by a team of notables in that genre including Dorothy Sayers, G. K. Chesterton, and Agatha Christie. Each wrote a chapter that follows logically from the clues presented in the preceding one. Their task was to come to one dénouement. At the end of the book the ideas of each contributor are compared to those of the author of the last chapter. The possibilities for use in an interactive classroom are many, provided that the level of the students is sufficient for them to follow the clues.

You, the reader, are given the license to join the author in his commentary about the characters in this story – until you find yourself caught up in the same predicament, with your own survival in question. Under such circumstances, the text you are reading is transformed into a discourse in which you have become an active participant. It is immaterial that you may never find yourself in a similar situation in real life. What is important is that the literary artist has involved you in this one. Your skill at reading the French language used by Maupassant has led you beyond the informational dimension to consider what you might say to negotiate your own preferences in the depicted transaction and how you might see yourself portrayed among the characters in the story.

This same procedure applies to the entire range of creative literature in the languages usually taught as foreign languages throughout the world. In *Faust,* to cite an example from German literature, the reader can be invited to participate in the fantasy of reliving a long-lost youth with the opportunity to choose a second time from the options that life normally offers only once. Pirandello places the reader (or the onlooker, when his plays are staged) in the company of those people who attempt to discover who their neighbors are and what they are doing in *Così è se vi pare* (*Right You Are if You Think You Are,* as the title goes in English). How would you handle the situation of being accosted by a mugger or a bandit? In Valle-Inclán's *Juan Quinto,* the priest protects himself from robbery by refusing to take seriously the efforts of the young man who is trying to be a bandit. It is difficult to be successful as a thief if one's intended victim will not play the part. A similar strategy is employed by Hoederer in Sartre's *Les mains sales* when he faces down his would-be assassin, Hugo. Of course, you, the reader, might not choose to engage in such dangerous ploys in a similar situation, but in following your own course of action, you enter into the creative act as modeled by the writer.

A more familiar plight to most readers might be that of the main protagonist of Ernesto Sábato's *El tunél.* Driven to anger and frustration over what he perceives as the loss of his loved one's affection, he writes her a nasty letter. After mailing it he has a change of heart and wishes that he never vented his rage in such a way. Since the letter was certified, he decides to retrieve it from the post office. But, alas! He has lost the receipt. The episode involving him and the clerk at the post office will be vividly realistic to anyone who has struggled with the bureaucratic mind of public servants. Without the receipt, says the clerk, nothing can be done. The counterarguments flow with skill from our protagonist, who says that the rules have to be in keeping with logic and that the post office cannot force him to send a letter if he doesn't want to.

"Pero usted lo quiso" ('But you wanted to'), the clerk replies.

"¡Ahora no lo quiero!" ('And now I don't want to!') he shouts back.

"No me grite, no sea mal educado. Ahora es tarde." ('Don't shout at me, don't be so impolite. It's too late.')

"No es tarde porque la carta está allí" ('It's not too late because the letter is right there'), he screams, pointing at the basket full of letters.

The give-and-take continues, with our man (by this time we, the readers, have joined him in his frustration) offering other documents to prove that he is the one who wrote the letter and the clerk finding a way to deny him his wishes.

The very act of communicating is sometimes the subject of literature, as in *El cepillo de dientes (The toothbrush)* by Jorge Días. In this play, a husband and wife find their marriage falling apart due to an inability to communicate. They cannot move beyond the surface meanings of words. For example, the husband is led to look up *amor* ('love') in the dictionary. He finds the following entry:

amor: afecto por el cual el hombre busca el bien verdadero; *amor seco:* nombre que se da en Canarias a una planta herbácea. ('*amor:* affection through which man looks for the the true good; *amor seco:* the name given in the Canary Islands to an herbaceous plant'.)

The wife has dreams in which objects have human feelings:

Anoche soñé con un tenedor. Debe ser un símbolo sexual inconsciente. Pero lo raro era que el tenedor decía que quería ser cuchara. El pobre tenía complejo de cuchara, de cuchara de postre. ('Last night I dreamed about a fork. It must have been an unconscious sexual symbol. However, the strange thing was that the fork said that he wanted to be a spoon. The poor thing had a spoon complex – a dessert-spoon complex'.)

At one point the husband announces that he is going to have a baby. This news is so shocking that his wife begins to address him with feminine forms: ¡No sea tonta! ('Don't be stupid!').

El cepillo de dientes is an example of theater of the absurd. How can such a literary piece be of use in an approach to foreign-language teaching supposedly based on realistic interaction? Although scenarios should replicate real-life situations, from time to time it is good to allow students to fantasize. By projecting themselves into imaginary roles or into unreal situations where basic elements of the human condition are brought into relief, students are free to say and do things in scenarios for which they might never want to assume responsibility.

Suggested procedures for the classroom

We have identified two major goals to accomplish in the teaching of literature in a second language: (1) to relate the particular text to a genre

114

and/or stylistic period and (2) to turn the text into a discourse that involves the reader. The first goal is best attained by working toward the second one. In the process, matters of form and style in the text should become as meaningful to the second-language reader as they were for the reading public to which the text was originally addressed. Of course, the appreciation of literature may entail a number of other goals. The two stated here, however, are considered to be fundamental to an interactive approach to literature and may even be important components in other approaches. Two procedures for accomplishing these goals are outlined below. The overriding concern in both procedures is to keep learners aware of the text as a sample discourse about matters of importance to the people who speak the language in which it was written. Literary texts are preserved by these people because they consider them worth repeating in some way. If we do our job properly in the classroom, these texts will be re-created once again as discourse, and our students will respond in a way analogous to the community of readers, listeners, or spectators who were willing to make them part of their literary heritage.

Procedure 1: Discourse before text

This procedure is favored because it closely follows the way that texts originate, namely as real or imagined human interactions. The students' first task is to work through a scenario based on the theme of the reading selection. They are not exposed to the text until all three phases of strategic interaction have been completed. Following the final phase of debriefing, the literary piece is assigned as homework reading. At the next class meeting, the students discuss how the author handled the theme. They are asked for their opinion about the outcome reached by the author. Attention is also drawn to the mechanics of the text. What stylistic devices were used? How successful were they? How has the text been affected by the structure of the target language (or, in Vygotskyan terms, in what ways was the author "object-regulated")? Once the text has been analyzed in terms of its status as discourse, the discussion can turn to the question of how the cultural background of the author and the intended public affected understanding of the text. The final series of questions to pose deals with how the piece fits with other literary creations of its time. Students may be asked to compare this work with others by the same author or in the same period.

The process of moving from discourse to literary appreciation can be conceived of as movement through a layered structure, with discourse at the nucleus surrounded by separate layers of text, cultural background, and literary appreciation (Figure 7.1). This set of concentric circles is an appropriate image to use here because it configures the way

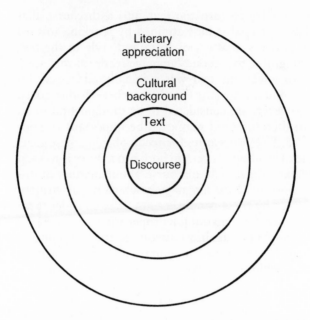

Figure 7.1   A layered view of discourse activities

in which each activity encompasses the preceding one and stands progressively farther away from actual discourse.

The progression from discourse to literary appreciation can be illustrated by working through a scene from Ionesco's play *Rhinocéros*. This play is about a man who is going through a very disconcerting metamorphosis: He is turning into a rhinoceros. A friend of his attempts to console him by downplaying the changes that are becoming increasingly harder to ignore. Before assigning the text for reading, a scenario like the following can be given to the students:

Role A: Recently you have been unable to sleep well. You feel hyperactive during the day. Your friend is a physician. Ask him/her to make a diagnosis of your ailment.

Role B: Your friend has symptoms of hypochondria. He/she expresses a concern about having a serious illness. However, there appears to be no reason for alarm. Since you are a physician, your friend has come to have a consultation with you. Prepare yourself for this consultation.

It is likely that player A will recount the symptoms in a straightforward way, and player B will have to give the diagnosis in a reassuring manner. The relevant dialog in the play takes place between Jean (the victim of the metamorphosis) and Bérenger (the friend), in which the friend attempts to console the victim. Ionesco's original text is simple enough for beginning students:

Jean: Je ne me sens pas très bien! ('I don't feel very well!')

Bérenger: J'en suis désolé. Qu'avez-vous donc? (I'm sorry. What's wrong?')

Jean: Je ne sais pas trop, un malaise, des malaises... ('I don't know. Some discomfort, uneasiness.')

Bérenger: Des faiblesses? ('Do you feel faint?')

Jean: Pas du tout. Ça bouillone au contraire. ('Not at all. Actually, I'm bubbling over with energy.')

Bérenger: Je veux dire... une faiblesse passagère. Ça peut arriver à tout le monde. ('I mean... a passing faintness. That could happen to anyone.')

Jean: A moi, jamais. ('Not to me.')

Bérenger: Peut-être un excès de santé, alors. Trop d'énergie... ('Perhaps you have too much health, too much energy...')

The humor of the scene increases as more symptoms are introduced and Bérenger continues to play the solicitous friend. Having already had the experience of generating a discourse on the same topic, students are given a vantage point from which to view Ionesco's text as an alternative treatment of a matter that is familiar to them. Even more importantly, their attention can be drawn to elements of discourse that are not represented in the written text, such as intonation, facial expressions, gestures, and body motions. How are the two roles to be executed? Is Jean in such a depressed state that his lines are spoken with falling tones? Does he keep his eyes lowered and his face expressionless? On the contrary, he may be on the verge of hysteria – an interpretation that may be more in keeping with his supposedly hyperactive state.

Once the class has reached some agreement on how the text represents a possibly real discourse, attention can shift to how cultural background may affect interpretation by a native French public. Certainly the metaphoric attributes that people assign to animals are part of culture. For example, wisdom is given to the owl by English speakers while in China and other Asiatic countries, the monkey is endowed with that quality. In Ionesco's play, the rhinoceros is seen to be energetic and even frisky. For English-speaking students, the same animal may appear dimwitted and, although powerful, rather slow to respond to stimuli. As a result, North American students may find Jean's symptoms to be more suggestive of a young colt than a rhinoceros. If we fail to point out this difference in animal metaphor, we may lead our students to an interpretation of Ionesco's play that is less than complete.

Having investigated all matters of cultural background that might affect the public's expectations, we are ready to enter the final stage in the treatment of the play. We started with discourse and proceeded to the text placed in its cultural matrix. We involved the students actively in performing a scenario built on a related theme. In doing so, we provided an opportunity to address all potential difficulties of language form and use. Our work took on an increasing degree of aesthetics as we next invited the class to draw comparisons between Ionesco's text and potential performances of it. We are now prepared to consider the play as a literary piece. How does it express the genre we have come to know as "theater of the absurd"? What are its salient characteristics and how does it compare with other plays by Ionesco, such as *The Bald Soprano*? The most significant question to pose in this last stage is the following: In what way is *Rhinocéros* worthy of preservation as a work of literature? To answer the question, at least in part, requires that we look once again at how Ionesco constructed his text, how he used language to build the particular form of humor that derives from absurdity. The experienced teacher of literature will certainly have much to cover in this final stage. It is good to point out that this procedure as well as the others discussed below do not dictate a particular viewpoint or school of literary analysis. The emphasis is on the approach and the motivation remains that of showing how students can be made to experience the literary text through interaction. It is in the diverse types of experience (in scenarios, in discussing the text as discourse, in analyzing the literary piece with the teacher's guidance) that we help students achieve self-regulation.

Procedure 2: Text before discourse

This procedure takes the class through the same stages as in the first procedure, with the exception that the text is given to the students before discourse is developed. In following this procedure, the students are led to respond to the text as an object before developing any other kind of regulation. After having done the reading, groups of students are formed to create a derivative scenario. Putting the text first may be useful when there are several possible themes that may yield scenarios. A novel, for example, may have several plots and subplots unfolding from chapter to chapter. Separate groups of students may choose to focus on different ones, all equally valid. In this procedure, as in the first one, the teacher must make a decision of how much text to give the students as a chunk. Sometimes, self-contained episodes are evident in the text, such as the "bishop's candlesticks" episode in *Les misérables* or the Gretchen episode in *Faust*.

Using the opening chapter from the popular novel *Raiders of the Lost Ark* by Campbell Black (1981), we can prepare an assignment for ESL/EFL students that illustrates how this procedure might work. We begin by assigning the first chapter for out-of-class reading (the chapter describes a meeting between two men working in the German SS during the Second World War). We accompany the reading with questions that direct attention to the three dimensions of conversational interaction set forth in Chapter 1 (information exchange, transaction, and interaction), such as:

A. Information exchange:
　1. Who are the people involved in this episode?
　2. What matter of business brings them together?
B. Transaction:
　1. What are the reactions of each to the matter at hand?
　2. What key words or phrases does each use in attempting to dominate the discussion?
C. Interaction:
　1. What relationship do the two men have to each other?
　2. Do you feel any sympathy for either of them?
　　 Why or why not?

The answers can be discussed in class, so that the author's particular way of depicting the three dimensions can be brought out.

The next step is to form groups of students and charge them with re-creating the scene as a new scenario in different settings. Instead of a military outpost in wartime, it can be a business office in peacetime. The charge given by the senior officer to the junior officer can be changed from locating an elusive specialist in archaeology to convincing a talented scientist to join the research department of the firm. In completing this assignment, each group is required to work on all roles of the scenario as a unit. The teacher should make certain that the students are engaging all elements (roles, setting, character portrayal) that were presented in the original reading selection.

Background information as part of scenario preparation

Keeping uppermost in mind the need to build interaction with the text, the teacher may find a discussion of cultural background is useful as part of scenario preparation. If, for example, a scenario is to be constructed on the Ugolino episode of Canto XXXIII of Dante's *Inferno*, then some explanation may be necessary in the early stages. Students accustomed to a view of hell as fire and brimstone may be surprised to find that in Dante's conception, the deepest, most vile part of the underworld is cold and covered with ice.

Finding literature that fits the life of the students

The problem with contrasts in cultural background is reduced considerably when the literary pieces chosen reflect the interests and concerns of the students themselves. Such a fit between life and literature can be shown in the choice of American literary texts for ESL students. The United States has been called a nation of immigrants. Almost every group to arrive on its shores has contributed to its literary heritage. American authors write more commonly than it might seem about the experiences of making a new beginning; of the difficulties in adjusting to new patterns of living; and of the alienation from family, friends, and the ways of the home country. As Newman (1980) has pointed out, American literature has developed "horizontally," with the same motifs being repeated in different ways over the years. The result is that each succeeding generation of Americans can find themes in literature that somehow apply to their own condition. Having to deal with cultural differences is a major one. Recall how Hawkeye, the American frontiersman in James Fenimore Cooper's *The Last of the Mohicans,* must explain the ways of the Indians to a British army officer who is totally ignorant of such matters. Similarly, in Nathaniel Hawthorne's *The Scarlet Letter,* the Indians conclude incorrectly that the large red letter A on the breast of the main female protagonist must mean that she is a very important person in the community. When Washington Irving's Rip Van Winkle awakes from his long sleep, he finds a society that has changed considerably from the one he knew.

In spite of all appearances, the most serious problems of the newly arrived in the United States are not broken hot water taps or undependable public transportation. The newcomer must decide on how to be a person in a society that has different ways of defining its roles. The daily life of any immigrant or refugee is, at best, an uncertain one and, at worst, a struggle against indignities. Young Paul, in Pietro DiDonato's *Christ in Concrete,* was as much alone in looking for work in the New York of 1939 as many young people of today who find themselves cut off from family and friends as they search for a position in the new world.

ESL students in North America, as well as in other English-speaking countries, are caught up in a saga of new beginnings that is the stuff of literature. For such students, working through novels, short stories, and poetry that treat the same saga can be not only instructive but therapeutic as well. One is less alone in a new land where the experiences shared by those who came before can be related to one's own life. In some cases, teachers can build on themes treated in current literature that deal with specific problems of their students. The following scenario was built on the film *El Norte* about Central Americans who come to the United States to find work.

Scenario Title: **Opportunity Knocks But Once**

Role A: You and your younger sister (or brother) have recently moved to the United States from Guatemala. You have a hard, low-paying job but were recently offered a new job that would double your current salary and give you a chance to advance. The one restriction is that you must travel to Chicago to take the job and you must come by yourself. Your sister (or brother) is not well and has just entered the hospital. What will you do? Prepare to discuss this matter with your sister (or brother).

Role B: You and your brother (or sister) have recently moved to the United States from Guatemala. You have both found work but you had to resign because of poor health. In fact, you are now in the hospital. It is unpleasant there for many reasons, especially because you do not speak English well. You can be released from the hospital if you can prove to the doctor that someone will take care of you at home. Discuss this matter with your older brother (or sister) who lives with you.

With EFL classes taught in non-English-speaking countries, one cannot draw as effectively from the experience of relocation because the student body has not been separated from its home culture and society. Even in these circumstances, literature is valuable because it enables students to create a world with language beyond isolated sentences. Widdowson (1981) argues that the choice of literary pieces should be made, as much as possible, in terms of how each extends the human experience of the learners. A more eloquent statement of the theme of this entire chapter could hardly be found.

Summary

The gap between skill and content courses in second-language education has been long recognized by the profession. It is not realistic to postpone the teaching of content until all basic skills are acquired. In an interactive approach to second-language literature, the text is viewed as discourse. By constructing scenarios based on the theme of the text, students can be involved in the act of creation in much the same way that the author was.

Two procedures are offered in this chapter as ways to approach the teaching of literature. In the first, students work through a scenario based on the text. After they have completed the three strategic inter-action phases, they are allowed to read the text and discuss it. In the second procedure, the text is given to the students before they develop a discourse from it. When the societal mindset of the text differs significantly from that of the students, the teacher may have to create scenarios that replace the original circumstances with those of contemporary times. Whenever possible, it is good to find texts that reflect the experiences of the students.

8 Language use in the strategic interaction classroom

In this chapter, the details of a strategic interaction lesson are described, in order to demonstrate how an interactive approach can be inaugurated in a class of second-language learners who have been following a standard audiolingual approach. First, however, we will consider the nature of classroom discourse in general, in order to provide a backdrop for the demonstration.

The two major functions of language in the strategic interaction classroom

The functions of language in the strategic interaction classroom fall into two general categories: pedagogical and performance. The pedagogical category is the more diversified of the two. It includes explaining, describing, critiquing, and evaluating, and typifies language use in rehearsal and debriefing. Either the native or the target language may be used to execute these functions. The performance category includes all strategic functions and requires the use of the target language. At the outset of instruction, the target language is restricted to the performance phase. Rehearsing and debriefing must be done in the native language in order to assure that input to the students is comprehensible. As time passes and the class develops greater proficiency in the target language, this language can take over some of the pedagogical functions. Ideally, the final stages of the course of instruction will find students using only the target language for both pedagogical and performance functions. The dynamics of language choice are weighted in favor of the target language, since the students will find it easier to stay with the target language in all functions as they gain confidence in it.

This approach to the use of the target language contrasts rather sharply with the one inherited from the audiolingualism of the 1950s. According to customary audiolingual practice, all activities in the classroom should be conducted in the target language right from the start. The following exchange will sound familiar to many teachers. It was taken from a real class meeting at the University of Delaware in 1984:

123

Teacher: ¿De dónde eres, Nicholas? ('Where are you from, Nicholas?')
Nicholas: Uhm...uh...
Teacher: ¿De dónde eres? ('Where are you from?')
Nicholas: Uh...I know what you're saying, but...
Teacher: Nicho*las!*
Nicholas: Uh...
Teacher: (*looking at another student*) Enrique, ¿de dónde eres? ('Enrique, where are you from?')
Enrique: Soy de los Estados Unidos. ('I'm from the United States.')
Nicholas: (*looking around at his classmates and laughing nervously*) Heh, heh...

Silence reigns in the classroom while this exchange is taking place. Nicholas's inadequacy to respond to what should have been a simple question is on display to the entire class. An Enrique always seems to be present to make Nicholas and others like him feel even more inadequate. In the thinking of the inflexible audiolingual teacher, Nicholas has committed a major sin. He tried to defend himself in his native language. His argument that he understood but could not respond in Spanish fell on deaf ears. The teacher has ignored Nicholas's appeal for help in order to keep the Spanish-only game going.

We can explain Nicholas's behavior in Vygotskyan terms. By answering the teacher in English, he was attempting to gain control over the object (represented by the Spanish language). For him, as well as for the remainder of the class, the teacher plays the part of the "other." By soliciting her help, he signaled to her that he wanted her to fulfill the regulatory function that goes with the "other." Her refusal to do so revealed that she preferred to let the conversation be controlled by the object. In classrooms regulated by the object, few students – even the ones who respond correctly to the dictates of the object – will manage to develop self-regulation and the fluency that comes with it.

The following is another authentic dialog showing object-regulation, even though an effort was being made to address functions in the target language:

Student 1: Tome las regletas azules. ('Pick up the blue rods.')
Student 2: (*picks up some blue rods from the table*)
Teacher: ¿Es correcto? ('Is it correct?')
Student 3: No, it should be *toma.*
Teacher: ¿Qué quiere decir *it should be?* ('What does *it should be* mean?')
Student 3: Oh...debería ser *toma.* ('Oh, it should be *toma.*')
Teacher: Muy bien. ('Very good.')

The transcription does not do justice to how student 3 actually delivered his last line. He did not make the slightest effort to sound like a speaker of Spanish. With her *Muy bien,* the teacher rewarded him nonetheless for his use of the target language to make the grammatical commentary. She chose to ignore the student's clear understanding that his commentary was in the category of pedagogical function and not performance. Although the student appealed to the teacher's role of "other," the teacher preferred to respond in terms of the "object." Even so, the heavily accented comment of the student indicated that he was not abandoning his attempt to move away from object-regulation.

Comprehension and production

The observation that comprehension appears to precede production in first language acquisition has led some methodologists (e.g., Asher 1977) to hypothesize that students of any age learning a second language should be taken through the same sequence, sometimes with extended periods of time during which no production is allowed. There is reason to question both the explanation for comprehension before production in a first language and its application to second-language learning. An alternative interpretation of why first-language learners seem to understand before they can produce speech may be found in the slower rate of motor development related to speech production over the rate of cognitive development. Perhaps children would speak earlier if they could manage the necessary articulations.

Even if it could be argued that comprehension should precede production in second-language learning, there is no way to determine how long the interval between the two phases should be sustained. In situations like those of the group scenario, where there is no rehearsal and comprehension does not come via a verbal message (see Chapters 2 and 3), production in the target language may be provoked through participation in an event with others. In applying the so-called input hypothesis to the second-language classroom, Krashen (1982: 21) advises teachers to strive for meaning first, with structure to be acquired later. In the context of strategic interactions, the following adjustment is made: Strive for interaction first, then meaning, and finally structure. It is even possible that not all interactions lead to the kind of "semantic" meaning intended by Krashen. In an article entitled "The benefits of poor communication," Kursh (1971) points out that we engage in many interactions where meaning is either veiled or misdirected. The shouting matches that sometimes take place between two drivers involved in an auto accident would be examples of a kind of "poor" communication. Neither party really listens to the content of the discussion and, in fact, can rarely remember afterward just what was said. A social benefit is gained, nevertheless, since each has discharged the tension that has been created by the situation.

125

The primacy of meaning in communication has been questioned by others. As early as 1935, the anthropologist B. Malinowski rejected the view of language function as the expression of thought or the communication of ideas (see Frawley and Lantolf 1984). As Frawley and Lantolf observe, people's belief that they understand each other when they communicate is likely to be more important than the actuality of understanding. The primary purpose for communication may well be control – not only over others but also over objects and oneself. If knowing can be identified as the act of individuals, it finds its beginnings in the social interaction of groups. The significance of thought as a social act is borne out in the context of second language acquisition. Generating monologs is a far more difficult task for the learner than conversing with others. In the interactive approach thought grows from dialog and then becomes private and internal to the individual. The path of learning a new language should naturally follow the same path, from publicly induced thought to a personally internalized one.

The discourse of a sample strategic interaction lesson

With the foregoing discussion as background, we are ready to observe how a group of second-language learners developed meaning through the execution of a scenario. The following is a transcription of the discourse generated in the rehearsal, performance, and debriefing of a scenario in a second-semester class in Italian at the University of Delaware in the spring of 1985. There is no intention here to dictate what must be done. The author substituted for the regular teacher to show how strategic interaction can be introduced into a standard audiolingual classroom. The unit from the textbook dealt with verb tenses, and the vocabulary was on the subject of travel. A video camera was used to record the activities of the class.

Script (transcribed from videotape):

Teacher: Oggi facciamo un esercizio di un incontro di due persone in Italia. E' un esercizio per aiutarvi a imparare i tempi verbali.

(*Commentary*: The teacher begins by telling the class that the work for the day will be about a meeting of two people in Italy and that it will help them learn the verb tenses. The teacher subsequently went on to review the tenses. The purpose of this introduction was to establish a bridge between what was supposedly learned before the strategic interaction lesson and what will be treated now. Judging from the reaction of the students, practically no interest is shown in verb tenses. Some students stare vacuously at the floor. Others look away. Only four or five of the thirty-odd students display attentiveness by establishing eye contact with the teacher. After approximately five minutes of questions and answers about verb tenses the teacher starts the rehearsal phase for the scenario.)

Teacher: Allora, dividetevi in gruppi.

(*Commentary*: The teacher asks the students to divide up into working groups. The students move around and form groups of seven to eight. The teacher moves around the room, distributing slips of paper with the roles of the scenario. Two groups are arbitrarily designated as "A" groups and two as "B" groups.)

Teacher: I want you to read your roles and I will circulate around to help you. You will find that these roles are different. Each is special and you will have to anticipate what the other side will say.

(*Commentary*: The teacher switches to English in order to assure that the students understand what they are to do and what they should anticipate in the ensuing interaction with other groups. The scenario roles written on the slips of paper are as follows.)

Ruolo A: Un amico italiano ti ha prestato la sua macchina per fare una gita a Perugia. Purtroppo, non conosci bene i regolamenti stradali italiani e preferisci che l'amico ti accompagni. Come convincerai il tuo amico ad accompagnarti a Perugia?

Ruolo B: Hai prestato la tua macchina ad un amico americano che vuole andare a Perugia. Ma dopo di aver promesso la macchina, uno zio ricco di Lucca ti telefona per dirti che ti comprerà una nuova macchina se tu porti i tuoi genitori a fargli una visita lo stesso giorno in cui hai promesso la macchina al tuo amico. Cosa gli dirai?

Role A: An Italian friend has lent you his car to take a trip to Perugia. Unfortunately, you are not acquainted with Italian traffic laws and you prefer that your friend go along with you. How will you convince him to accompany you to Perugia?

Role B: You have lent your car to an American friend who wants to go to Perugia. But after having promised him the car, a rich uncle from Lucca calls you to say that he will buy you a new car if you take your parents to visit him – on the same day that you promised the car to your friend. What will you tell your friend?

Strategic interaction

(*Commentary:* The groups display diverse patterns of interaction. In some, the students lean forward in a tight circle and engage in rapid and energetic talk.)

Script of group talk:

Student 1: What car should we use?
Student 2: Fiat.
Student 3: No, no. A Ferrari. My new Ferrari. Ha! Ha!

(*Commentary:* Other groups are more pensive and less talkative. The teacher circulates among the groups making himself available to answer questions from the students. The rehearsal continues for approximately twenty minutes. At one point, the teacher goes to the blackboard and writes some expressions on it. He explains that these expressions can be used by the students during the performance in case they have trouble understanding the other party and want to ask their groups for help: *Non ti capisco* ('I don't understand you'), *Ripeti, per favore* ('Please repeat'), *Come si dice...* ('How do you say...'). The teacher then announces that the rehearsal phase has ended and the time has come for some performances. He asks for volunteers. When no one comes forward, he picks a student from a role A group and another from a role B group. He tells the remaining members of each group that they must be ready to offer any help or advice to their performing representative should he or she need it. The performance begins with the two students standing in front of the room. Nervous laughter is heard in the background. Student A looks down at some notes, mutters "OK" under his breath, and then looks up and speaks to student B. Word-level errors are underlined and phrasal errors are circled.

Script:

Student A: Buon giorno. ('Good morning.')

(*Commentary:* Student A gestures to student B as if to indicate that it is her turn to speak. Members of A's group laugh. Student B joins in the laughter. A takes on a serious air as he realizes that he must say more.)

Student A: Ti...piace...rebbe (inaudible) con mi...a un bevanda? ('Would you like (inaudible) with me to a drink?')

(*Commentary:* A's tempo of delivery is very slow and hesitant. He points at himself while saying *con mi* and then makes a gesture as if to drink something after saying *bevanda*. *Un* is underlined to signal that it should be made feminine to agree with *bevanda*. Both words are circled to indicate that the entire expression is incorrect in this context.)

Student B: Non ti capisco. Ripeti per favore. ('I don't understand you. Repeat, please.')

(*Commentary*: B smiles as she says these lines. She speaks in a louder voice than A and appears more self-confident. A decides to try again.)

Student A: Ti...piace...celebbe
con mi...e...av...
una...a...a...bevanda?

(*Commentary*: A has corrected *un* to *una* but is still trying to use an incorrect phrase to invite B to have a drink with him, ostensibly to prepare her for the favor he wants to ask about going to Perugia with him. He repeats his gestures – pointing to himself while saying *con mi* and then making the motion of drinking. Laughter comes from the class.)

Student B: Uhm...uhm...

(*Commentary*: B has finally understood A but is hesitant to respond. After a few seconds, she holds up her hand as if to signal that she is going to speak but then remains silent.)

Student A: Sì o nò? ('Yes or no?')

(*Commentary*: A gives the impression that he has acquired some confidence in the interaction. He smiles as he presses her for an answer.)

Student B: No...ma...Abbiamo una problema...uh...uh devo andare a Lucca con i mai genitori oggi...per visitari un zio...lo zio ricco ...di Lucca...lo...mio...zio...è...ricca e...e...uh...e... ('No...but...we have a problem...uh...uh I have to go to Lucca with my parents today, to visit an uncle...the rich uncle... of Lucca...my...uncle...is...rich...and...and...')

(*Commentary*: At this point, B turns to her group for help.)

Student B: (*to her group*) Come si dice *promise*? ('How do you say *promise?*')

(*Commentary*: Someone in group B answers her, but it is inaudible beyond the small circle.)

Student B: Promesso? ('Promise?')

(*Commentary*: B turns back to face A and continues her explanation of why she cannot go with him to Perugia.)

Student B: e...uh...e...ha promessato se io vado a Lucca, mi darà una macchina nuova...un Ferrari, un Ferrari rossa. Mi molto dispiace ...ma ma...devo andare a Lucca oggi...per...per...per...i... uh...per il mio Ferrari nuova a prendere. Devo andare a Lucca.

('and...uh...and...he has promised if I go to Lucca, he will give me a new car...a Ferrari, a red Ferrari. I am very sorry, but but...I have to go to Lucca today...for...for...for...the... uh...for my new Ferrari to get (it). I have to go to Lucca.')

(*Commentary*: There is laughter from the class as she mentions "Ferrari." B's tempo of delivery picks up as she finishes her explanation. She terminates her discourse softly and smiles. More laughter from the class. A grimaces and remains silent. He shakes his head in a negative fashion and looks down at his notes. He extends his right hand as if to mark the onset of speech but says nothing. He then looks in the direction of his group. Several students from group A speak almost simultaneously.)

Student from Group A: Domani. ('Tomorrow.')

(*Commentary*: A turns back to face B but remains silent. He points to himself and then to B. His period of silence continues for approximately fifteen seconds more. B looks back at her group. The remainder of the class is restless but no one says anything. Finally, A begins to speak.)

Student A: Vo...vorresti〔venire fatto〕un gita...a...a...a...Perugia...uh ...('Would...would you like to come make a trip...to...to...to... Perugia...uh...')

(*Commentary*: A appears to be searching for the right word. A student from A's group repeats the word *domani* 'tomorrow.')

Student A: Domani? ('Tomorrow?')
Student B: Ripeti per piacere. Non ti capisco. ('Repeat, please. I don't understand you.')
Student A: Vorreste <u>venire</u> <u>fatto</u> <u>un</u> gita a... ('Would you like to come make a trip to...')
Student B: Una gita a Perugia? ('A trip to Perugia?')
Student A: Sì. ('Yes.')
Student B: Domani? ('Tomorrow?')
Student A: Sì, domani. ('Yes, tomorrow.')
Student B: Sì, va bene...va...bene...uh...ma...oggi...devo andare a Lucca ma domani...uh...__ ho niente da fare...no...niente da fare. Domani...uhm... ('Yes, all right, all right...but today...I have to go to Lucca but tomorrow, uh, I don't have anything to do. Tomorrow...uhm...')

(*Commentary*: B turns to her group for help.)

Student B: Come si dice *will have*? ('How do you say *will have*?')
Student in group B: Avrò... ('I will have...')
Student B: (to A) Domani avrò la macchina nuov...nuova...e...

〔guardiamo〕a Perugia con la...la...la mia macchina nuova. ('Tomorrow, I will have the new car...and we will drive to Perugia with the...the...my new car.')

Teacher:	(to student A) Sei contento? ('Are you happy?')
Student A:	Sì. ('Yes.')
Student B:	Bene! ('Good!')

(*Commentary*: The performance is concluded and the students rejoin their groups. The teacher comes back to the front of the class.)

Teacher: I think you were both very good. You got your points across. You made a rearrangement, right? And it seemed to work. Uh...What are some of the other things you (student A) could have said when you found out that she couldn't lend you the car?

(*Commentary*: Teacher looks at group A. A student speaks.)

Student:	He could have gotten mad.
Teacher:	He could have taken the bus.
Another student:	Una motocicletta. ('A motorbike.')
Teacher:	But I think you worked it out very well. Uh...Just a few things came up...*Problema,* even though it ends in an *a,* it is one of those words that is masculine in Italian. It probably should be feminine, but it isn't.

(*Commentary*: Teacher turns and writes a phrase on the blackboard: *E' un problema* ('It's a problem'). He continues talking about the errors he noted in a relaxed, nonthreatening way.)

Teacher: You ought to make a note of that. By the way, write these things down if you think they will help...Uh, you used the *passato prossimo* (present perfect) beautifully, except...uh... *promettere,* to promise, (which) is one of those irregular verbs which goes to *promesso.* It's like *mettere,* 'to put,' whose past participle is *messo.* And, uh *Ferrari*...in Italian all automobiles are feminine...*una Ferrari, una Lancia, una Maserati, una Lamborghini,* even though Lamborghini, Maserati, and Ferrari are the names of people who designed the cars...When we refer to the car, we say...*la...la mia Ferrari.*

(*Commentary*: The teacher continues the debriefing, covering other errors, such as the irregular verb forms *piacerebbe* – with *r,* not *l* – and *vorresti,* for second-person singular, as opposed to *vorreste,* which is the second-person plural. He elicits the correct way to say "drive a car" – *guidare una macchina* – and points out that this expression would not be the usual one to say "We will go together to Perugia," which should be *Andiamo assieme a Perugia.* The debriefing period lasts about twelve minutes and is terminated by the end of the class hour.)

During an interim of several class periods, the teacher reviewed the conversation generated by the students and prepared an edited version of it. No effort was made to polish it to make it seem like a written text. The conversational format was preserved. Only the grammatical errors were removed. This edited version was brought back to the class and the students were given the opportunity to read it over. As a reminder of what they had said in their initial performance, a videotape of it was shown. The edited transcript was as follows:

A: Buon giorno. Ti piacerebbe venire al ristorante con me per bere qualcosa? Sì o nò?

B: Nò. Abbiamo un problema. Devo andare a Lucca con i miei genitori. Devo andare oggi per visitare mio zio ricco di Lucca. Mi ha promesso – se io vado a Lucca – chi mi darà una macchina nuova, una Ferrari Rossa. Mi dispiace molto, ma devo andare a Lucca.

A: Vorresti fare una gita a Perugia domani?

B: Domani?

A: Sì, domani.

B: Va bene. Oggi vado a Lucca ma domani non ho niente da fare, ed avrò la macchina nuova. Possiamo andare insieme a Perugia.

A: Bene.

The opportunity was provided for questions. All students in the class were then asked to practice the two parts. As the students rehearsed, they were encouraged to use the edited dialog only as a reference point. They were not to read it. After five to ten minutes of rehearsal, the original role players were asked to perform their parts again. The following is a transcription of this second performance.

Script:

A: Buon giorno.

(*Commentary*: A looks briefly at his paper and then drops it before speaking. He establishes eye contact with B before speaking.)

B: Buon giorno.

(*Commentary*: B does not look at her paper. She, too, has established eye contact.)

A: Ti piacerebbe venire al ristorante con mi per bere qualcosa, sì o nò?

(*Commentary*: A points to himself, as in the first performance, when he says, "con mi." However, he does not repeat the gesture of drinking.)

B: Nò...abbiamo un problema...devo andare oggi a Lucca con i miei genitori per visitare mio zio ricco. Mi ha promesso...se io vado oggi a Lucca...mi darà una macchina nuova...una Ferrari rossa. Mi dispiace molto ma devo andare oggi a Lucca.

(*Commentary*: B's delivery is rapid but articulate. She does not glance at her paper at any time, but while she is speaking, A looks at his several times.)

A: Vorreste <u>fadere</u> una gita a Perugia domani con la macchina nuov<u>o</u>?
B: Domani?
A: Sì, domani.
B: Domani, non ho niente da fare ed avrò la macchina nuova. Possiamo andare insieme domani a Perugia.
A: Bene!

Some observations about student performances

The most evident difference between the first and second performances of the scenario is the considerable reduction in errors. It is apparent that the students involved in producing the discourse were especially eager to give their utterances as much grammatical accuracy as possible. After all, it was a discourse that they themselves created. The implication for the teacher is that accuracy can indeed grow from a setting that encourages fluency as the first goal to attain. Occasional "reruns" of scenarios will allow students the chance to sharpen their control over the mechanics of language use. Direct observation of the two performances shows a marked reduction in object-regulation in the second one. Both students used gestures during the second performance that supported what they were saying instead of replacing it (as in A's motion in the first performance of drinking something when inviting B to have a drink). A comparison of the edited text with the actual performance in the rerun clearly shows that both students were attempting to communicate creatively. For example, A added the phrase *con la macchina nuova* ('with the new car') in his offer to postpone the trip to Perugia. He does make a mistake of gender agreement, using the masculine form of the adjective instead of the feminine, but such a mistake is probably not a reflection of a lack of competence on his part since he clearly demonstrates at other points in the conversation that he knows about gender agreement. His attempt at pronouncing a flapped *r* in *fare* resulted in the production of *fadere*. I, as the teacher, must take the blame for this mistake because I tried to help him by pointing out the similarity between the Italian flapped *r* and the intervocalic *t* and *d* in English words like "latter" and "ladder."

Evidence of the creation of meaning through interaction comes in the first scenario when it becomes clear to A that he cannot use the strategies prepared by him and his group during rehearsal. B will not be able to accompany him and A struggles to find something to say. The word *domani* becomes the key to resolving the problem. It infers the remainder of the conversation, that is, the chance to go together to Perugia in B's new car. The word *domani* has more than the lexical meaning of 'the day after today.' Since it has been used to resolve a dilemma, it has taken on a strategic meaning as well. After the second performance, I asked the class to pick out the most important word in the entire dialog. Without any hesitation, they agreed on *domani*. The word is not likely to be forgotten soon because it was part of a negotiated settlement. It will carry its strategic potential for the learners well into other encounters.

Evaluation

The rise of any new approach to second-language instruction leads inevitably to the question of evaluation. Determining the progress made by second-language learners has never been easy, and the profession has witnessed the development of several types of tests over the years. With audiolingualism came the so-called discrete-point tests still in popular use. Cloze-type tests were next to rise to prominence on the grounds that they preserved context and presented the target language in a natural framework of a text or a spoken discourse. Most recently, the FSI oral interview has attracted much interest. Since the interview requires exchanges in the target language, it resembles more closely the customary form of conversation. Aside from having to assess each student individually, the FSI test is still oriented around elements of structure that do not include the personal style of transaction or the presentation of roles that people experience in real life. In addition, the levels of proficiency set in the interview are idealized and open to subjective interpretation. Nevertheless, its elicitation of active performance by the learner makes it more suitable for the interactive classroom than either the discrete-point or the cloze test.

What is missing in all three types of tests is consideration of the ties of each language user to a community of speakers. As a participant in such a community, the second-language learner may become an effective communicator without satisfying the specifications of an idealized native speaker. The interactive classroom, with its group work and unfettered scenario performances, is a kind of speech community. The effectiveness of each student-member to function within this community should be assessed by means that reflect the social use of language. The levels of fluency and accuracy should be gauged in terms of persons playing comparable roles in real-life communities where the target language is spoken. These roles may even include the ones played by articulate nonnative speakers.

There are three potential evaluators in every interactive classroom: the teacher, the students evaluating each other, and each individual student doing a self-evaluation. Various procedures can be developed to allow the results of the three evaluations to be used by the teacher, as chief evaluator, in arriving at a composite assessment of each student.

It is to be expected that each teacher will weigh each aspect according to his or her particular views. The idea is to attain an overall measure of achievement by assessing student performances in a number of different settings and situations. To aid in making a record of student performances, selected scenarios can be recorded, either on audiocassettes or on videotape. It is useful for each student to listen (or watch and listen) to a playback of his or her own performances. Each playback can be discussed not only in terms of the skills they reflect but also with regard to where improvement is needed. The advantage of using three different evaluators lies in the special viewpoints that each brings to bear on assessment.

1. *The teacher as evaluator.* The teacher is probably the best equipped to evaluate the way roles are portrayed and how cultural conventions are followed in the performances. As the semester passes, the teacher may move from a rating scale with three points to a five-point scale, as more is known about each student's capacities. Other matters for the teacher to assess are detail of solutions to scenarios, the effectiveness of these solutions in the interaction, and the intelligibility of the performance itself.

2. *Students as peer evaluators.* Students are also likely judges of originality and intelligibility. Although teachers should be prepared to consider several possible alternative solutions to scenarios (since they may have witnessed the scenario being enacted on previous occasions), the students may have a better feeling for how their fellow learners have used their limited resources. Since students have a more limited knowledge of the target language than the teacher, they tend to be concerned more with grammatical errors and mispronunciations.

3. *Students as self-evaluators.* Each individual student is best prepared to answer the following questions: Could I have used more of my vocabulary? Could I have requested more help from the teacher? In other words, students know better than anyone else how well they have utilized what they know about the target language.

The features of student performances in scenarios along with the major responsibilities for evaluating are set forth in Figure 8.1. It is wise for the teacher to arrange conferences with groups of students to discuss the separate evaluations each has made. The teacher can then come to an evaluation that is a composite of the three.

Perhaps the safest observation that can be made about assessing student achievement is that performance on any test reflects how each student has put his or her competence to work in a particular instance, under a very particular set of circumstances, to respond to a particular request for performance. Almost every canon we have formulated about

Performance features	Major evaluation by:		
	Teacher	Peers	Performer
1. Role portrayal	√		
2. Cultural conventions	√		
3. Originality	√	√	
4. General intelligibility	√	√	
5. Grammatical accuracy	√	√	
6. Pronunciation		√	
7. Use of vocabulary			√
8. Use of teacher help			√

Figure 8.1 Chart for evaluating student performances in scenarios

testing can somehow be challenged. For example, do students actually perform better when they are talking about subjects familiar to them? Lantolf and Khanji (1983) report on the differences in spoken discourse of an ESL student when subjected to a structured oral interview and when allowed to speak freely about a topic of his own choice. The nonstructured discourse of the student was marked by more parataxis than syntaxis. That is, the student was less syntactically accurate in free discourse but more fluent. Whereas he displayed more grammatical accuracy in the structured oral interview, he did not generate as much discourse. Lantolf and Khanji's findings lead us to question the notion that the structured oral interview is a reliable way to assess students' fluency in a second language. In addition, it is clear from the performance of the student that performance in a second language is as variable as performance in a first language.

We must remember that when we create any kind of test or install any kind of evaluation procedure, we do it on the presupposition that testing is a legitimate way to assess achievement. All language tests, even the pragmatically sensitive ones, put aside some aspects of how people use language in order to concentrate on others. Perhaps the best indication of second-language learning and acquisition comes long after the course of instruction has ended and the teacher discovers that some students have built on what they experienced in the classroom to become users, in some way or another, of target language.

Summary

Language use in the classroom falls under two major categories: pedagogical and performance. The target language is introduced via the performance category and is subsequently spread to the pedagogical functions. In customary audiolingual classes, target-language use is often for display purposes. Students tend to remain overly regulated by the object. Whatever method is applied in the classroom, efforts should be made to help the learners achieve self-regulation in the target language. In an interactive approach, it is the enactment of scenarios that leads to self-regulation. The precedence of comprehension over production is questioned in this chapter. An alternative to this notion is that meaning is created in interaction. In order to provide an illustration of how meaning is created in interaction, the discourse generated by the implementation of a scenario is presented and analyzed. The class is taken through the three phases of rehearsal, performance, and debriefing. At a subsequent class meeting, the role players are asked to repeat their performances after going over an edited version of it. The second encounter is marked by a considerably reduced number of errors. Most importantly, the players do not repeat the script verbatim. Instead, they use it as an aid to the enactment. The chapter concludes with some observations about evaluation. The proposal is made that evaluation of progress be shared by the teacher with the students, who are asked to evaluate each other and themselves. It is pointed out that each of the three evaluators brings a special viewpoint to the assessment of progress. The chapter concludes with the suggestion that the best proof of learning is reflected in how well each student builds on the experience of the formal instruction after it is completed.

9 Training teachers in strategic interaction

This final chapter offers guidance to those teacher trainers who wish to conduct workshops in strategic interaction. The contents of the chapter are drawn from the personal experiences of the author in holding workshops in several locations both within the United States and abroad.

A checklist for workshop preparation

It is useful to gather as much information as possible beforehand about the workshop participants and their immediate needs. The following checklist is intended to help organize this information:

(1) Who will the participants be?
_____ teachers
_____ superintendents
_____ teacher trainers
_____ student teachers
(2) What is the purpose of the training?
_____ to cover basic techniques of the approach
_____ to concentrate on how to address one of the skills (reading, writing, etc.)
_____ to prepare materials for classroom use
_____ to cover the theoretical foundations of the approach
_____ to train supervisors of teachers
_____ to prepare teacher trainers
(3) What will be the format of the training sessions?
_____ indicate length of time (a day, a week, two weeks)
_____ experiential mode (with demonstrations and group participation)
_____ formal presentations by speaker
_____ group discussions
(4) Will there be a follow-up?
_____ site visits by someone in charge
_____ reports to be filed by participants at a later date
(5) How will the workshop be evaluated?
_____ by a questionnaire filled out at the conclusion
_____ by a group of outside observers
_____ by the supervisor

The workshop should be opened with a few succinct remarks about the basic ideas of an interactive approach to language, second language acquisition, and roles in the classroom. These ideas can be summarized as follows:

1. Language is a tool for communication as well as a body of rules and words to learn.
2. Second language acquisition is an inherent ability in humans, but it requires interaction with others through the target language in order to be activated.
3. The classroom is to be a speech community where students cooperate with each other in the work of learning. The teacher's cooperation requires the playing of several different roles (e.g., consultant, coach, guide, information giver).

Next, the scenario should be introduced as a central pedagogical device through which interaction is channeled in the target language. Rather than launch into a detailed presentation of the workings of the scenario, however, it is preferable for the participants to execute one themselves. The most effective training sessions I have conducted have included some sort of experiential mode. By actively engaging in the workings of scenarios, the trainees get an inside view of the advantages to learning that are inherent in the strategic interaction approach. Student volunteers from the classes of the teachers in attendance may also be used, but it is preferable to save student demonstrations until after the workshop participants have done their own scenario. The trainer may choose to use a first-day scenario (as in Chapter 2) with a language that is unknown to the participants or a two-role scenario executed in a language that they teach. If the participants are supervisors who are not engaged in language teaching, the trainer may use scenarios that treat the kinds of interactions these supervisors customarily have with teachers or with parents of students enrolled in language classes. In a 1980 workshop for bilingual teachers conducted in Texas for the Dallas Independent School District, I used a multiple-role scenario involving a monolingual English-speaking principal of an elementary school, a bilingual Spanish-English classroom teacher, and a monolingual Spanish-speaking parent. The scenario dealt with the frequently felt need to share vital information among the protagonists about an injury sustained by the child of the monolingual Spanish speaker. The realistic nature of the scenario helped illustrate its value as a pedagogical device. After performing the scenario (in which all participants spoke either Spanish or English as they normally would), the group discussed not only the outcome but also the circumstances that surrounded the use of each language. One outcome was a better understanding of the specific ways that communication across language boundaries could be improved in the bilingual school.

Whatever special interests workshop participants might have, they should be taken through the three phases (rehearsal, performance, and debriefing) and then allowed to discuss what they have experienced. They should be encouraged to consider the ways this experience relates to their own setting.

Another important component of almost all strategic interaction training sessions is the guidance given for how to prepare one's own scenarios. The trainer may choose to arrange the participants in groups to try their hand at writing scenarios suitable to their needs. When the scenarios have been completed, they can be tried out by other groups and then critiqued by all in attendance (see Chapter 3 for guidelines on scenario writing).[1]

Questions likely to be asked in training sessions

The trainer can expect that at least some of the following questions will come up during the training session.

(1) *Doesn't the teacher have to be very fluent in the target language in order to help the students prepare scenarios?* Teachers who are not native speakers of the target language sometimes worry that their own limitations will embarrass them before their students. No one, not even a so-called native speaker, can know everything in a language. The nonnative teacher can anticipate some of the things students might want to say beforehand and then prepare target-language equivalences. After a scenario has been used several times by different groups, the teacher will have a fairly clear idea of what is likely to be asked. In the event that the teacher is totally unable to provide the correct target-language expression for what students want to say, the teacher should admit ignorance and then help the students find something else to say. Students are likely to develop a new degree of respect for a teacher who takes the trouble outside of class to find the particular word or phrase they were seeking and then gives it to them at the next class meeting.

(2) *Shouldn't students already have learned the basics of the target language before being exposed to strategic interaction?* Although the strategic interaction approach can be introduced at any level of instruc-

---

1 For teachers working in bilingual education programs, the Dallas Independent School District has prepared a *Bilingual Education Teachers Training Packet*. This publication contains a section on strategic interaction prepared in large part by Olga Rubio of IDRA (San Antonio, Texas) and Margarita Calderón of the National Training Resource Center (San Diego State University, San Diego, California). Those interested may obtain Packet II, Series B, from the Center for the Development of Bilingual Curriculum, Dallas Independent School District, 3700 Ross Avenue, Dallas, Texas 75204 USA.

tion, it is actually preferable to have students start off with it. In this way, they will learn the "basics" without being overly regulated by grammar and the use of the target language by the teacher. The second chapter of this book suggests a way to use strategic interaction right from the start of instruction.

(3) *Isn't the use of the native language in rehearsal and debriefing counterproductive to learning the target language?* Ever since the "audiolingual revolution" of the 1950s, the use of the learner's native language has become anathema in the classroom. The reaction was, of course, to the grammar-translation method that preceded audiolingualism. In grammar translation, the native language was used to the extent that translation to and from the target language was part of the learning expectations. The first point of difference between strategic interaction and grammar translation regarding use of language is that translation is never a required part of performance. The use of the native language is restricted to preparing and debriefing scenario performances. As time goes on, the teacher should encourage target-language use in rehearsal and debriefing, as well. Use of the native language in the second-language classroom is primarily to ensure intelligible input during the learning process. When competence in the target language becomes sufficient for use in all rehearsal and debriefing functions, the native language can be fully discontinued.

(4) *How much acting ability does the strategic interaction teacher need?* Although strategic interaction highlights the "drama" of interaction, it does not require that the teacher be an actor or engage in histrionic activities. The drama, as we have seen in Chapter 3, results from the performing of scenarios. It is internally felt by the performers rather than externally modeled by the teacher. Learners perform for their own benefit, and the strategic interaction teacher is free to develop a personal pedagogical style which may or may not be construed as dramatic. In brief, the dramatic playing of roles by the teacher is not a requirement for strategic interaction.

(5) *How can the strategic interaction teacher be certain that control over classroom activities will be maintained during the three phases?* Not occupying center-stage at all times does not mean that the teacher no longer directs the activities of the classroom. Teacher involvement is present in all three phases of strategic interaction. It is the teacher who sets up the scenario by distributing the roles to individual groups. It is also the teacher who provides guidance and help throughout the rehearsal phase. It is the teacher, again, who determines when performances should begin and how long they should last. Finally, the teacher takes center stage in the debriefing phase to lead the discussion of performances. Actually, the question is not one of teacher control but rather

141

of teacher management of activities. The students themselves must take control of their own learning – with the help of the teacher whenever needed.

(6) *How do I gain confidence in this new approach?* Confidence – or lack of it – can be a major factor in the second language classroom for the teacher, as well as the students. Students sometimes enter the program of instruction with what Stevick (1976: 51) has called "an elevated level of anxiety." Students may feel that their classmates know more than they do at the outset. The teacher may be concerned about setting tasks that are too difficult for the students. The growth of confidence in the teacher about the approach as well as in the students about their abilities with the language comes with the stimulation of target-language discourse. The more students are able to say in the target language in their efforts to resolve an issue or a dilemma, the more they will appreciate the teacher as a resource person. The teacher, in turn, cannot help but become more comfortable with an approach that builds self-motivation in the students.

(7) *Should students be told about the approach to be used in the course?* Telling the students that the methodology is innovative might have mixed results. On the one hand, it might reduce initial anxiety in facing the new experience (Stevick 1980). On the other, it might draw attention to how the class is being conducted instead of keeping the students focused on what is to be learned. In any event, a distinction should be made between telling the students what they are expected to do (i.e., making the methodology clear to them) and how the methodology is constructed. People who are enrolled in a course of language study expect to learn the target language. The methodology will become clear to them as they proceed. The issue is not whether they approve of the methodology but rather how much of the target language they have learned by the end of the course. If they feel that they have somehow fulfilled their expectations, they will probably laud the teacher and the method. If they have not, they will most likely have criticisms for both. In either case, not much insight will have been gained into the second-language learning process. It may be best not to tell students about the methodology unless they need to know this information in order to decide among several alternative courses being offered.

(8) *What should the teacher do if members of the class do not take the methodology seriously?* Such a situation can develop regardless of the approach followed by the teacher. Students may begin to joke among themselves instead of rehearsing scenarios, for example. My answer to apparent lack of interest by the students is to give them the option of returning to an approach used formerly. They can be given grammar exercises and readings, but it would be much better if the teacher would find the patience to help them interact with other members of the class.

The teacher should not worry about comparing strategic interaction students with others on any of the skills. Khanji (1983) is one source to be consulted on the results of a comparison of strategic interaction with other approaches. Some students sincerely believe that the drill-and-exercise methodologies are the best ones. This belief may even be culturally imbued. These students feel that if they do not suffer in the learning process, they are not learning. They praise the stern taskmaster. It is not uncommon to hear such students remark that the teacher was very good but they were very bad learners.

(9) *How do age and personality factors affect learning through strategic interaction?* With all the research done on the subject, we are not close to an understanding of how age and personality affect second-language learning. The question does come up at times with regard to the appropriateness of scenarios in strategic interaction. Some teachers have expressed a concern that their students may be too old (or too young) for scenarios. Or they may worry about shy students being unwilling to stand in front of the class. Actually, strategic interaction permits a range of diverse behaviors to be manifested among students. The so-called shy students find refuge in the group while the more assertive ones volunteer to be the group representative in the performance phase. Students are not required to play the representative until and unless they are ready to do so. As far as age is concerned, scenarios have been used with a broad range of grade levels, from elementary school to university and beyond. The drive to interact does not appear to be constrained by age. What is significant is that the theme of the scenario be made to fit the general interests of people at their particular age levels. Subjects that interest children (e.g., bargaining over a favorite toy) are no more likely to inspire adults to interact than adult subjects (such as bargaining for a raise) would enthuse a child. Whatever the age, interaction brings into play the same strategic dimension and the same psychological need for role portrayal.

(10) *In what way can strategic interaction be called a "personalized" approach?* Strategic interaction gives students the opportuntity to express their own social and psychological needs through a new language while they are in the process of learning it. There is no promotion of one learning style over any other. The three phases of strategic interaction provide ample opportunity for students to learn in their own ways. Working in groups assures that no single style of learning is imposed on all others.

There is another way in which strategic interaction is personalized: It relates the target language to the real life of learners through the use of scenarios. Interactions with vendors, doctors, officials, and relatives in the lives of the students and the teacher are probably not unlike similar interactions among people living in the target culture. A good exercise for participants in workshops is to ask them to contemplate how these interactions might be carried off in the target language. Doing so keeps everyone aware of how cultural and psychological factors influence personal language use. Although second-language teachers have long been exhorted to bring realism into their classrooms, rarely have they been asked to focus on life's interactive aspects. Life is nowhere as drab or matter-of-fact as it is sometimes depicted in the artificial conversations of textbooks. For ESL teachers, the availability of an English-speaking community in which her students must function is a special aid not available in settings where the target language is foreign to the surrounding community. Since ESL students must function daily in the language they are studying, it is not difficult for the teacher to create scenarios based on authentic happenings. In some strategic interaction classrooms, students have even written their own scenarios, based on events that have involved them personally.

(11) *How important is knowledge of theory to the second-language teacher?* Second-language teachers are usually very busy people, with little time to read or even think about linguistics and the general principles of language acquisition. Perhaps theory is only for those methodologists who have managed to extricate themselves from the daily grind of the classroom and can ponder such matters at their leisure. But theory *is* important for the practitioner. Without it, the teacher is caught up in a never-ending search for new activities and routines to provide to an audience of students who seem constantly to be on the brink of boredom. Some knowledge of theory keeps the teacher from being a hopeless eclectic, doing things blindly and without any full understanding of what is going on in the learning process. Yet it is not enough just to tell teachers and teacher trainees about theory. To be fully effective, theoretical statements should be related to phenomena that teachers observe firsthand in the classroom. Therefore, taking a clue from the strategic interaction approach, I have tried to get workshop participants involved in looking for answers to familiar questions such as the following:

1. Why do some students complain that they can only understand the teacher and none of the fluent speakers of the target language?
2. Why is it so hard for my students to retain vocabulary?
3. Why do some of my "best" students have difficulty engaging in free conversation?
4. Why can't my students ever seem to learn all the grammar, even when I cover it so thoroughly?

Many other questions occur to the practicing teacher, but for purposes of illustration we will entertain only the four given here. The first question compels a consideration of the conditions under which the students have been exposed to the language. Strategic interaction recognizes the essential communal use of language. Interaction in groups facilitates the acquiring of tolerance for a range of speech styles and pronunciation, even when the variation is nonnative. The dynamics of speaking in groups cannot be activated when the teacher dominates all exchanges with the students. It is not a compliment to the teacher to be told that the students understand no one else. Instead, it is a sign that more group interaction should be undertaken in the classroom.

The question of vocabulary retention is as old as the language teaching profession itself. In strategic interaction theory, words are like currency that students exchange with each other in order to give meaning to their actions. In such a context words have value for their users. Of course, there is always an attrition of vocabulary whenever it is not used – but the same holds true for words in the students' native language. If the fall-off of vocabulary is drastic, then the reason may stem from the way in which it was presented. Decontextualized lists of words can be learned quickly, but just as quickly they can be forgotten. Words searched for and used in context are retained much longer by the learner. During scenario preparation and rehearsal, the teacher should not give the students lists of so-called useful words. If given such a list, students are likely to conclude that these words must somehow be used. Their attention is drawn away from achieving the goal of the scenario and toward the words chosen by the teacher as important. It is far more useful to let the students look up whatever words they might need in a dictionary. In this way, students feel that they are commanding the vocabulary instead of the vocabulary commanding them.

Some students always excel in the artifact-based exercises of traditional foreign-language instruction yet seem to be unable to transfer this knowledge to actual conversations. When this condition is prevalent in the classroom, the teacher can suppose that the course is overly regulated by the grammatical artifact. In the absence of the give-and-take of conversation and the opportunity to develop self-regulation, transfer from mechanical drills is difficult, if not impossible. (See, however, Danesi 1985 for some lively examples of how to address grammatical matters in the format of a game.)

Grammar can never be learned fully. But more importantly, it must not be considered the equivalent of acquiring second-language competence. In strategic interaction, grammar is more like an output than an input. Its value lies in what learners make of it and can apply to understanding and generating utterances. "Covering" grammar is not to be equated with learning it. The teacher who is keyed only to coverage is not automatically attuned to what the students are learning. The evidence of student learning is found in their performances in the target language.

Suggestions for organizing a teacher-training workshop

Although individual teacher-training workshops should be tailored to the particular needs of their participants, the major points of the strategic interaction approach can usually be covered in six steps:

1. *Introduction.* The teacher trainer makes some general remarks about the background of the strategic interaction approach. These remarks should be short, so that the participants are not overburdened with theory before they witness the practice of strategic interaction.
2. *Activity with scenarios.* The participants are organized into working groups and put through the experience of rehearsing, performing, and debriefing scenarios assigned to them by the teacher trainer. If possible, the themes of the scenarios should relate to the participants' work situations.
3. *Discussion of scenario activity.* Participants should be led in a general discussion of each phase of scenario work. They should be asked to comment on their own performances and what they would expect their students to produce under the same set of circumstances.
4. *Scenario composition.* The participants should be told about the essential features of an effective scenario (such as role pairing, ambiguity, and dynamic tension). Then they should divide into small working groups to compose scenarios for use in their own classes.
5. *Performance of participants' scenarios.* After the teacher trainer has helped each group prepare its scenarios, the groups should exchange scenario roles and peform each other's scenarios. In this way, the participants will have the opportunity to judge the effectiveness of their own creations and to make any adjustments needed in them.
6. *Final critique.* Participants are led in a final critique of the strategic interaction approach, the preparation and use of scenarios, techniques in evaluation of student performances, and appropriateness to the classroom. Some means should be found to reproduce scenarios for everyone in attendance. As a follow-up to the workshop, the teacher trainer should ask the participants to report on their use of scenarios and the students' general reactions to the strategic interaction approach.

The distribution of time

The relative weighting of each of the six steps in the workshop is flexible and depends to some extent on the judgment of the teacher trainer and the particular needs of those in attendance. However, the following distribution of time has been found to provide sufficient coverage of each step. The time allotments are spread over an eight-hour workshop.

(1) Introduction: ½ hr. or 6.25% of time
(2) Scenario activity: 1 hr. or 12.5% of time
(3) Discussion: 1 hr. or 12.5% of time
(4) Composition: 2 hrs. or 25.0% of time
(5) Performance: 1½ hrs. or 18.75% of time
(6) Final critique: 2 hrs. or 25.0% of time

    Totals: 8 hrs. or 100% of time

Summary

Workshops and inservices are popular ways to train educational personnel (administrators as well as teachers) in new approaches to second-language instruction. The organizer of a strategic interaction training program should ascertain who the participants will be and what their immediate needs are. Decisions should be made beforehand about the format for the training sessions and how long each should last. Follow-up helps determine how effective the training program has been. A good way to expose the participants to strategic interaction is to allow them to experience the process of preparing and performing scenarios themselves. The themes of the scenarios can be made to fit their special interests and needs. Answers are provided for ten questions about strategic interaction that commonly arise in workshops and inservices. The chapter concludes with some suggestions about how to organize a strategic interaction workshop.

This book closes with an invitation to teachers to let me know about their experiences with strategic interaction. The approach is still in its infancy and there is much mutual benefit to be gained from sharing information about the ways it is being implemented in the classroom. I would be delighted to hear from you.

References

Abbs, B. 1980. *Communicating Strategies*. Longman, London.

Anthony, E. 1963. "Approach, method and technique." *English Language Teaching* Vol. 17, pp. 63–7.

Asher, J. 1977. *Learning Another Language through Actions: The Complete Teacher's Guidebook*. Sky Oak Productions, Los Gatos, Cal.

Bakhtin, M. 1981. *The Dialogic Imagination*. Ed. by M. Holquist. University of Texas, Austin.

Berne, E. 1972. *What Do You Say after You Say Hello?* Bantam, New York.

Bernhardt, E. 1985. "A model of L2 text reconstruction: the recall of literary texts by learners of German." *Delaware Symposium VII*. To appear in Labarca and Lantolf (in press).

Bickerton, D. 1984. "The language bioprogram hypothesis and second language acquisition." In W. Rutherford (ed.), *Language Universals and Second Language Acquisition*, pp. 144–61. John Benjamins, Amsterdam.

Brown, J. 1985. "¡Diga! Telephone protocols and strategies in the intermediate Spanish conversation course." *Hispania* Vol. 69, pp. 413–17.

Bruffee, K. 1984. "Collaborative learning and the conversation of mankind." *College English* Vol. 46, pp. 635–52.

Brumfit, C. 1980. "From defining to designing: communicative specifications versus communicative methodology in foreign language teaching." *Studies in Second Language Acquisition* Vol. 3, pp. 1–9.

Burke, K. 1973. *The Philosophy of Literary Form*. University of California Press, Berkeley.

Carrell, P. 1982. "Cohesion is not coherence." *TESOL Quarterly* Vol. 16, pp. 479–88.

Carrell, P., and J. Eisterhold. 1983. "Schema theory and ESL reading pedagogy." *TESOL Quarterly* Vol. 17, pp. 553–73.

Christensen, C. 1981. *Teaching by the Case Method*. Harvard Business School, Cambridge, Mass.

Crandall, J., T. Dole, N. Rhodes, and G. Spanos. 1985. "The language of mathematics: the English barrier." *Delaware Symposium VII*. To appear in Labarca and Lantolf (in press).

Crookall, D. 1985. *Simulation Applications in L2 Education and Research*. Special issue of *System* Vol. 13, no. 3.

Curran, C. 1976. *Counseling-learning in Second Languages*. Apple River Press, Apple River, Ill.

Dalbuono-Glassman, E., and F. Bosco. 1982. *Profili*. Forest House, Washington, D.C.

Danesi, M. 1985. *Language Games in Italian*. University of Toronto Press, Toronto.

de Beaugrande, R. 1984. "Writer, reader, critic: comparing critical theories as discourse." *College English* Vol. 46, pp. 533–59.

DiLaura (Morris), S-J. 1983. "Teaching without grammar: title XII experience at the University of Delaware." *FL Annals* Vol. 16, pp. 339-42.

Donato, R. 1985. "A psycholinguistic rationale for group activity: empirical evidence." *Delaware Symposium VII.* To appear in Labarca and Lantolf (in press).

Edmonson, W. 1981. *Spoken Discourse: A Model for Analysis.* Longman, London.

Elgin, S. 1980. "Never mind the trees: what the English teacher really needs to know about linguistics." *University of California Bay Area Writing Project Occasional Paper No. 2.* Berkeley, Cal.

Faerch, C., and G. Kasper (eds.). 1983. *Strategies in Interlanguage Communication.* Longman, London.

Frawley, W. 1987. *Text and Epistemology.* Ablex, Norwood, N.J.

Frawley, W., and J. Lantolf. 1984. "Speaking and self-order: a critique of orthodox L2 research." *Studies in Second Language Acquisition* Vol. 6, pp. 143–59.

Freundlich, J. 1981. "No thyself: the art of refusal." Paper delivered at the international TESOL conference, Detroit, Mich.

Giles, H., and P. Smith. 1979. "Accommodation theory: optimal levels of convergence." In H. Giles and R. St. Clair (eds.), *Language and Social Psychology.* University Park Press, Baltimore, Md.

Goodwin, C. 1981. *Conversational Organization: Interactions between Speakers and Hearers.* Academic Press, New York.

Grice, H. P. 1975. "Logic and conversation. The William James Lectures, Harvard University." In P. Cole and J. Morgan (eds.), *Syntax and Semantics,* Vol. 3, *Speech Acts.* Academic Press, New York.

Guiora, A., and W. Acton. 1979. "Personality and language behavior: a restatement." *Language Learning* Vol. 29, pp. 193–204.

Halliday, M., and R. Hasan. 1976. *Cohesion in English.* Longman, London.

Hartwell, P. 1985. "Grammar, grammars, and the teaching of grammar." *College English* Vol. 47, pp. 105–27.

Heath, S. 1983. *Ways with Words.* Cambridge University Press, New York.

Jacobson, R. 1984. "College teaching by the 'case method': actively involving students is the aim." *Chronicle of Higher Education* Vol. 28, pp. 17, 20.

Johnson, P. 1982. "Effects on reading comprehension of building background knowledge." *TESOL Quarterly* Vol. 15, pp. 169–81.

Jones, K. 1982. *Simulations in Language Teaching.* Cambridge University Press, Cambridge.

Jones, L. 1983. *Eight Simulations.* Cambridge University Press, Cambridge.

Khanji, R. 1983. "Two innovative methods in foreign language teaching: their effects on the acquisition of interactive skills." Ph.D. dissertation, University of Delaware.

Krashen, S. 1982. *Principles and Practice in Second Language Acquisition.* Pergamon, New York.

Krashen, S., and T. Terrell. 1983. *The Natural Approach.* Pergamon, Oxford.

References

Kursh, C. O. 1971. "The benefits of poor communication." *Psychoanalytic Review* Vol. 58, pp. 189–208.

Labarca, A., and R. Khanji. 1986. "On communication strategies: focus on interaction." *Studies in Second Language Acquisition* Vol. 8, pp. 68–79.

Labarca, A., and J. Lantolf (eds.). In press. *Proceedings of Delaware Symposium VII*. Ablex, Norwood, N.J.

Lantolf, J. 1984. "From theory to practice: methodological eclecticism." Plenary lecture at the Second Symposium on Developments in Language Learning, Pennsylvania State University.

Lantolf, J., and W. Frawley. 1983. "Second language performance and Vygotskyan psycholinguistics: implications for L2 instruction." *The Tenth LACUS Forum*, pp. 425–40. Hornbeam Press, Columbia, S.C.

Lantolf, J., and R. Khanji. 1983. "Non-linguistic parameters of interlanguage performance: expanding the research paradigm." *The Ninth LACUS Forum*, pp. 457-72. Hornbeam Press, Columbia, S.C.

Lantolf, J., and A. Labarca (eds.). 1987. *Research in Second Language Learning: Focus on the Classroom*. Ablex, Norwood, N.J.

Leeman, E. 1982. "Classroom discourse and linguistic intake." *New Yorker Werkstattgespräch*. Goethe Institute, New York.

Littlewood, W. 1981. *Communicative Language Teaching*. Cambridge University Press, Cambridge.

Maley, A. 1980. "Teaching for communicative competence: reality and illusion." *Studies in Second Language Acquisition* Vol. 3, pp. 10–16.

McClosky, S. 1984. "Teaching dramatic literature." *College English* Vol. 46, pp. 385-91.

McCreary, D. 1984. "Communicative strategies in Japanese-American negotiations." Ph.D. dissertation, University of Delaware.

McKay, S. 1982. "Literature in the ESL classroom." *TESOL Quarterly* Vol. 16, pp. 529–36.

Morris, S-J. 1987. "A field test of strategic interaction." In Lantolf and Labarca (1987), pp. 134–40.

Neufeld, G. 1979. "Towards a theory of language learning ability." *Language Learning* Vol. 29, pp. 227–41.

Newman, K. 1980. "An ethnic literary scholar views American literature." *MELUS* Vol. 7, pp. 3–19.

Oller, J. and P. Richard-Amato (eds.). 1983. *Methods That Work*. Newbury House, Rowley, Mass.

Pellegrini, A. 1984. "Effect of dramatic play on children's generation of cohesive text." *Discourse Processes* Vol. 7, pp. 57–67.

Phelps, L. 1985. "Dialectics of coherence." *College English* Vol. 47, pp. 12-29.

Puhl, C. 1987. "Integrating communicative and rule-based methodologies through the scenarios of Strategic Interaction." In Lantolf and Labarca (1987), pp. 141–9.

Quinn, T. 1984. "Functional approaches in language pedagogy." *Annual Review of Applied Linguistics 1984–85*, Vol. 5, section IV, pp. 60–80. Newbury House, Rowley, Mass.

Redeken, G. 1984. "On differences between spoken and written language." *Discourse Processes* Vol. 7, pp. 43–55.

Richards, J., and T. Rodgers. 1982. "Method: approach, design and procedure." *TESOL Quarterly* Vol. 16. Reprinted in J. Richards. 1985. *The Context of Language Teaching*. Cambridge University Press, New York.

Roberts, J. T. 1982. "Recent developments in ELT: Part II." *Language Teaching* Vol. 15, pp. 174–94.

Rubin, J., and I. Thompson. 1982. *How To Be a More Successful Language Learner*. Heinle and Heinle, Boston.

Rumelhart, M. 1983. "When in doubt: strategies used in response to interactional uncertainty." *Discourse Processes* Vol. 6, pp. 377–402.

Salah, G. 1983. *The Sequencing of Scenarios According to Complexity in the SI Method*. Ph.D. dissertation, University of Delaware.

Savignon, S. 1983. *Communicative Competence: Theory and Practice*. Addison-Wesley, Reading, Mass.

Scarcella, R. 1983. "Sociodrama for social interaction." In Oller and Richard-Amato (1983), pp. 239–45.

Schachter, J. 1983. "Nutritional needs of language learners." In M. Clarke and J. Handscombe (eds.), *On TESOL '82*, pp. 175–89. TESOL, Washington, D.C.

Scollon, R., and S. Scollon. 1981. *Narrative, Literacy and Face in Interethnic Communication*. Ablex, Norwood, N.J.

Seliger, H. W. 1983. "The language learner as linguist: of metaphors and realities." *Applied Linguistics* Vol. 4, pp. 179-91.

Semke, H. 1984. "Effects of the red pen." *FL Annals* Vol. 17, pp. 195–202.

Showstack, R. 1982. "Language teaching vs. language learning systems." *System* Vol. 10, pp. 179–89.

Stevick, E. 1976. *Memory, Meaning and Method*. Newbury House, Rowley, Mass.

Stevick, E. 1980. *Teaching Languages: A Way and Ways*. Newbury House, Rowley, Mass.

Tannen, D. 1984. *Conversational Style: Analyzing Talk among Friends*. Ablex, Norwood, N.J.

Titone, R. 1982. "Interaction in the language classroom: theories and research models." *Rassegna di linguistica applicata* Vol. 14, pp. 1–16.

van Ek, J. 1975. *The Threshold Level*. Council for Cultural Cooperation of the Council of Europe, Strasbourg.

Verity, D. P. 1985. "The making of a method: SI as discursive activity." Research paper for course on discourse in FL instruction, University of Delaware.

Vygotsky, L. S. 1978. *Mind in Society*. Harvard University Press, Cambridge, Mass.

Vygotsky, L. S. 1962. *Thought and Language*. MIT Press, Cambridge, Mass. Original Russian edition, 1932, Moscow.

Widdowson, H. 1981. "The use of literature." In M. Hines and W. Rutherford (eds.), *On TESOL '81*, pp. 215–29. TESOL, Washington, D.C.

Wilkins, D. 1976. *Notional Syllabuses: A Taxonomy and Its Relevance to*

References

Foreign Language Curriculum Development. Oxford University Press, London.

Wong-Fillmore, L. 1976. *The Second Time Around: Cognitive and Social Strategies in Second Language Acquisition.* Ph.D. dissertation, Stanford University.

Index

153